AF279155

Grey Heron surveying the Heron Pond at sunrise Bushy Park. Photo: Sue Lindenberg

First published in the UK in 2022 by Supernova Books, an imprint of Aurora Metro Publications Ltd. 80 Hill Rise, TW10 6UB www.aurorametro.com info@aurorametro.com
t: @aurorametro F: facebook.com/AuroraMetroBooks
West London Wildlife © 2022 Aurora Metro Publications Ltd.
Cover photograph © 2022 James Yates
Cover design: copyright © Supernova Books/2022 Aurora Metro Publications Ltd.
Editor: Laura Burgess

Photo credits and thanks to: Bushy Park & Home Park – Ian Rodger, Sue Lindenberg; Chiswick House – Ian Alexander, James Yates, Orangeaurochs, Patche99z; Crane Park – Friends of the River Crane Environment (FORCE) including Gary Backler the Chair and Trustee Board members Rob Gray, Alison Horwood and Catherine Wyatt. Steve Marshall / Wild Future, Caroline Duncan, John Waxman, Crane Valley Partnership; Darlands Nature Reserve, Totteridge – Roger Tichborne, Samuel Levy, Dudley Miles, Martin Addison; Dukes Meadows – Ian Alexander, Irid Escent, Kathleen Healy; Gunnersbury Triangle – Ian Alexander; Hampstead Heath – David Templer, David Wilson Cristiane Teston, James Ó Nuanáin, Alastairmck, Garry Knight, Neville Young, Ricardalovesmonuments, London Less Travelled;, Kew Gardens – Susanne Masters, James Yates, Wolfgang Stuppy, Patches99z, C T Johansson; London Wetland Centre, Barnes – London Wetland Centre, including Lisa.Woodward, Clara Wiggins, and Adam Salmon; Richmond Park – Friends of Richmond Park, including Vivienne Press, Janet Bostock, Christopher Hedley, and Roger Hillyer (Chair, Friends of Richmond Park). Amanda Boardman @mandsby, Eric Baldauf, Bartek Olszewski ONEWILDSHOT, Andrew Coleman, Kasia Ciesielska-Faber www.kasia.photography, James Kliffen, Diana Loch, Paula Redmond@pr_ultra; Riverbanks of the Thames - Phillip Briggs, Hugh Clark, Barracuda, John Chalmers, Kew Gardens, Kamran Safi, Carole Ratcliffe; Ruislip Woods & Lido – Ian Alexander; The Upper Thames Estuary - Thames Estuary Partnership, including Wanda Bodnar, Amy Pryor, and Chloe Russell. Panoramio, Jim Linwood, Neil Cummings, Mary Tester; Wimbledon Common – Ian Alexander, John Game, Amy Burgess, Andy Scott; back page, Garry Knight.
Printed by Short Run Press, Exeter, UK on sustainably resourced paper.
ISBN: 978-1-913641-30-6 (print)
ISBN: 978-1-913641-31-3 (ebook)

WEST LONDON
WILDLIFE

SUPERNOVA BOOKS

Red-breasted goose at London Wetland Centre: Photo: LWC

CONTENTS

London Wetland Centre. Photo: LWC

Roaring Red Deer Stag, adorned in bracken, during a rut in Bushy Park. Photo: Sue Lindenberg

"ONE TOUCH OF NATURE MAKES THE WHOLE WORLD KIN."

– William Shakespeare

Cormorant and Mute Swan at sunrise on Leg of Mutton Pond, Bushy Park. Photo: Sue Lindenberg

BUSHY PARK & HOME PARK

Ian Rodger

As part of the Thames flood plain, Bushy Park is a relatively flat parcel of land with deep sandy soils over clay. Spanning over 1100 acres, it is the second largest Royal Park after Richmond Park. It has a known historical occupation stretching back over 4000 years; bronze age barrows have been excavated near Sandy Lane and it still has a visible and extensive medieval ridge and furrow field system. Once three separate enclosed areas including a deer park and rabbit warrens, they were combined to become the Bushy Park we are familiar with in the early eighteenth century.

Due its use as hunting grounds since the 15th century and its unbroken evolution into a Royal Park, Bushy has a sizable population of trees which have been around for hundreds of years. There are approximately 400 veteran trees, of which 94 are considered to be ancient, and 196 are veteran Hawthorns. The classification of veteran indicates that the tree is considered old for its species and has a number of veteran features such as cavities, deadwood, cracks, holes, and heartwood decaying fungi. Once veteran trees reach a great age even for their species, they then become ancient veteran trees. In other words, all ancient trees are veteran trees, but not all veteran trees are old enough to be ancient.

So why are veteran trees important? Well, they add significant value to any landscape, due to their often-large sizes and curious forms, but they also have huge cultural and historical heritage. Many veteran trees have attained great ages due to being working trees, often pollarded to produce firewood or fodder for animals. Some even have connections to historic characters or past events, such as the magnificent Yew just upriver at Runnymede under which the Magna carta was signed in 1215. The process of cyclical cutting (pollarding/coppicing) used on working trees can extend their life dramatically; a Lime coppice at Westonbirt is an extraordinary example with an estimated age of over 2000 years. Probably most important of all their attributes is veteran trees' ecological value as deadwood habitats, which are now rare but once existed abundantly across Britain in the post-glacial wildwood. These varied habitat niches support rare fungi and associated saproxylic invertebrates whose larval cycles take place in several types of decaying wood. The cavities created by decaying wood provide habitat for nesting birds and roosting and breeding bats.

Wood decaying fungi and trees have evolved a complex relationship over millions of years of evolution. Most wood decay fungi are saproxylic, existing entirely on dead or non-functioning wood and are essentially recyclers, breaking down the

Fistulina hepatica. Photo: Ian Rodger

wood's structure and eventually reverting all the wood and tree detritus into soil. Certain fungi have adapted to grow in the inhospitable wet and oxygen deprived centre of the tree gaining the name heartwood decay fungi, such as Beefsteak fungus (*Fistulina hepatica*). These fungi are able grow in low oxygen environments and have developed enzymes to separate and dissolve the different components of the wood and consume them. Many heartwood decay fungi develop so slowly a healthy tree often grows new wood quicker than the fungi decays the non-functioning heartwood. This natural balance can be upset by external threats such as drought or aeration of the functioning structural wood via storm, or lightning damage. If the tree's energy is deviated away from new growth, it can lead to rapid progression of the decay fungi and subsequent structural failure and collapse.

Bushy Park has the oldest known dated tree in any of the Royal Parks: a Sweet Chestnut planted in 1370, making it over 650 years old. It has a trunk circumference of nearly 10 meters. Along Chestnut Avenue there are a number of wonderfully gnarled old veteran Lime trees full of cavities. Some are completely hollow and some are just sections of living remnants, demonstrating the survival capabilities of some trees. Further towards the west of Lion Gate is an area of old

Deer in the bracken. Photo: Sue Lindenberg

wood pasture which has some splendid veteran and ancient Oaks some of which are over 400 years old. One group has been fenced off, which has two main purposes. Firstly, to keep people away from the area under the tree to prevent compaction of the soil, and secondly to allow us to lower the risk of harm to the public from these elderly trees shedding branches or limbs. One particularly interesting area of the park lies to the west and south of Hawthorn lodge where there is an open area of bracken and numerous venerable Hawthorns, many of which are hundreds of years old. This is thought to have been used for deer coursing, hunting with dogs and, along with the scattered veteran Oaks, is a quite unique landscape feature. Ironically, the areas of bracken here are now used as cover and birthing areas for the deer.

All the veteran trees in Bushy are inspected every year as part of their tree management health and safety policy, and undergo a specialist veteran tree survey every five years where possible. These surveys assess the structural condition of the tree and its vitality. If the vitality is seen to be declining, they may look to revitalise the soil via decompaction and mulching with wood chip or other cultural practices. Part of the specialist survey is to identify associations with the trees and protect or enhance them. Young vigorous trees close by might provide too much competition or shade, so may have to be removed in a process called hallowing. However, smaller, less competitive trees are planted near veterans, especially Hawthorns, as their nectar when flowering helps to support the adult life cycle of many of the invertebrates existing within the trees. For example, the increasingly rare Cardinal click beetles (*Ampedus cardinalis*) and the False flower beetle (*Scraptia fuscula*), both make these trees their home.

A veteran oak in Bushy Park. Photo: Ian Rodger

A Gatekeeper butterfly. Photo: Sue Lindenberg

As trees age, they inevitably start to decline and decay as part of the natural aging process. Once they reach maturity, they often suffer storm damage and a gradual decrease in vitality related to their size and other environmental and biotic challenges. Often referred to as retrenchment or growing downwards, this is an adaptation the trees have developed to withstand their increasing height and girth, and balance them with diminishing resources through disfunction of the roots and xylem. Old maiden Oaks (un-cut) often form a new crown in their lower canopy and slowly withdraw resources from the upper sections which die back. This is known as stag heading and is a completely natural process. It allows the trees to carry on for many hundreds of years after re-distributing their energy assets and forming a better adapted structure, much shorter and stockier, giving it a natural resilience to the vagaries of the weather.

So, the veteran and ancient trees of Bushy Park not only provide great richness and aesthetic beauty to the visitor but also offer unequalled haven to a lush, often rare, and varied amount of precious wildlife.

Mute Swan on a frosty day in Bushy Park. Photo: Sue Lindenberg

A mackerel sky at sunrise in summer - Leg O' Mutton Pond, Bushy Park. Photo: Sue Lindenberg

Photo: Orangeaurochs

CHISWICK HOUSE

Ian Alexander

Chiswick's signature building, Chiswick House, was designed by Richard Boyle, 3rd Earl of Burlington, a keen amateur architect, and completed in 1729. He never intended to live in it: he owned the magnificent Burlington House on Piccadilly, now home to the Royal Academy. Like other wealthy English gentlemen, he had travelled to Italy on a Grand Tour to see its art for himself. He fell in love with Andrea Palladio's architecture, and on his return, built one of England's first Palladian villas to display his collection of paintings, furniture and souvenirs from his European travels.

While in Italy, Burlington met the English artist William Kent, and was so impressed that he brought him back to London to beautify his houses. Inside Chiswick House, Kent worked on the ornate ceilings. Outside, he designed the garden: his design became the pattern for the English landscape garden, complete with cascade and grotto, 'river', Palladian bridge, and fake temples to catch the visitor's eye. Palladian villas, landscape gardens, and Kent himself all became must-have fashion accessories for the man who had everything in the 18th century. The design created a fashion for wild-looking gardens with room for nature.

The cascade at Chiswick House

Chiswick House was inherited by the Dukes of Devonshire. It was said to be the favourite party-place of the fifth Duke's wife, Georgiana Spencer, the trend-setting but troubled ancestor of Lady Diana Spencer. She called the house 'my earthly paradise'. However, the house lost its glitz in the nineteenth century, and from 1892, Edward Tuke ran a mental health asylum in the building, using the wings as wards.

In 1929, the ninth Duke sold the house to the local council, who used it as a fire station. It became dilapidated during the Second World War, and in 1944 a V-2 rocket partly destroyed one of the wings. Threatened with demolition, the house was saved by the Georgian Group in 1948. The Ministry of Works (now English Heritage) took over the house and decided to return it to its original state, although they demolished the wings in 1956. Recent funding has led to further restoration of the house.

The extensive gardens around the house provide multiple wildlife habitats. Leaf-litter and dead wood support a rich variety of mini-beasts and fungi, including the bizarre white branches of the coral root fungus. The treetops echo with birdsong in springtime, from the familiar calls of blackbirds and robins to the sweet music of the blackcap and the song thrush. The 'river' is home to a wealth of waterfowl including Egyptian and Canada geese alongside nesting coots and ducks; herons stalk the shallows in search of frogs and small fish.

The obelisk and pond. Photo: Patche99z

Coral root fungus below a yew hedge in Chiswick House's gardens. Photo: Ian Alexander

Chiswick House's orangery houses an important collection of camellias. Some of them are centuries-old varieties that have become rare, and might well have been lost otherwise. Among them is the very first variety imported to Britain in 1794, *Camellia japonica* 'rubra plena'.

The local council managed the gardens, but lacked the funds to do much more than mow the lawns. Fortunately, the Kitchen Garden was maintained by a head gardener, supported by volunteers. I recall going along to dig, plant, and weed in the glorious vegetable, herb, and flower beds among friendly company: every task was a delight. If we were lucky, we'd be given some brightly-coloured rainbow chard to cook for supper. Once I had the job of making stem cuttings of whitecurrants, the rarer cousin of the blackcurrant and redcurrant. After we had planted out the desired rows of cuttings, all the volunteers were given a few cuttings to take home. My whitecurrant bush still flourishes, a tiny element in the Kitchen Garden's programme of conserving and promoting the enjoyment of old garden varieties.

Chiswick House Kitchen Garden. Photo: Ian Alexander

View of the gardens at Chiswick House. Photograph: Ian Alexander

The Chiswick House and Gardens Trust was formed in 2005, and the gardens were extensively restored to display the site's cultural heritage and natural beauty, and to provide better visitor facilities. Vistas not seen for a century suddenly reappeared in their 18th century splendour. Originally imported from Lebanon, the Atlantic cedars that frame the house have been admired by many visitors including the Shah of Persia and Queen Victoria. Recently, grafts were taken from the trees and shared with other historic gardens to help to ensure the future health of the species.

Caruso St John designed an elegant modern café where the stables once stood, with attractive spaces to eat and drink both inside and outside. This has added to the appeal of the house and gardens for locals who like to meet up or walk dogs in the grounds. The house is now popular as a party venue too, which is fitting as it was once the site of lavish entertaining by the 6th Duke (the 'Bachelor Duke'), who kept an impressive menagerie of exotic animals that included Sadi, an Indian elephant, monkeys and kangaroos. In 1844, he hosted a splendid banquet for Tsar Nicholas I of Russia. No expense was spared for the several hundred guests, who included Prince Albert and the King of Saxony. The summer parlour was entirely redecorated in the style of a medieval tent. "Where is the elephant?" asked the Tsar, but by then, sadly, Sadi had long passed away.

For more see: www.chiswickhouseandgardens.org.uk

Grey heron. Photo: James Yates

Swan on Upper Pen Pond, Richmond Park. Photo: James Kliffen

"IT SEEMS TO ME THAT THE NATURAL WORLD IS THE GREATEST SOURCE OF EXCITEMENT; THE GREATEST SOURCE OF VISUAL BEAUTY; THE GREATEST SOURCE OF INTELLECTUAL INTEREST. IT IS THE GREATEST SOURCE OF SO MUCH IN LIFE THAT MAKES LIFE WORTH LIVING."

– Sir David Attenborough

An Egyptian Goose enjoying a stretch by the Pump House Pond, in Bushy Park. Photo: Sue Lindenberg

River Crane. Photo: Crane Valley Partnership

CRANE VALLEY

Gary Backler

The River Crane is a small urban river, rising in the moat of Headstone Manor, Harrow, and flowing for around 35 km through West London to the Thames. Rivers are often of great importance for urban environments, as their flood valleys are where much of the remaining open spaces can be found. The Crane Valley contains around 2,000 hectares of open spaces, stretched out in green ribbons along the river system. These green corridors provide valuable green and blue habitats and routes for wildlife, linking together larger areas of green space into a nature network in the heart of suburban London.

Friends of the River Crane Environment (FORCE) was formed in 2003 to protect several small, open, riverside spaces in Twickenham from development. Some twenty years later, the community group has around 800 members, with a remit to protect and enhance hundreds of hectares of riverside open space, primarily south of Heathrow and the A30. Given the linear character of these spaces, much of their focus is on improving connectivity along the River Crane corridor, for both wildlife and human visitors.

River monitoring as part of the Citizen Crane project. Photo: FORCE

Purple loosestrife. Photo: FORCE

The River Crane itself has been heavily engineered over many years. It has been straightened, dredged, and toe-boarded, and the lower river has been put into a deep, wide, concrete channel. Wildlife needs variety in order to thrive, and this engineered approach removed many habitat niches and opportunities, aggravating the effects of the river's 'flashiness' and reducing its diversity. Over the last ten years FORCE volunteers have under-taken a number of projects to reverse this trend.

They have helped to remove hundreds of metres of toe-board and created new deflectors within the river to narrow its width and create more diversity. These have led to the development of more pools and riffles in the main channel, creating cleaner gravels for fish spawning and seeing healthy river weeds such as Ranunculus and water crowfoot thrive for the first time in living memory. They have installed floating berms to soften the concrete banks and planted them with wetland species to promote biodiversity. Weirs have been removed or modified, to facilitate the passage of fish, and eel passes installed. New backwater and marginal areas have been created and planted with reeds, marsh marigolds and purple loosestrife.

These shallow water and reed beds are ideal habitat for fish fry, where they can hide from larger fish and retreat when the river is in flood. Shoals of chub, roach and rudd, as well as sticklebacks, are visible at many locations. Damselflies and dragonflies have returned to the river in large numbers.

In 2022, they delivered a field trial to remove a 30-metre section of the lower river from its concrete straitjacket. A backwater was created, with flood attenuation benefits, and the riverbank and channel re-naturalised. Early signs are that this is working well, with more fish and invertebrates in this area as well as large-scale public interest and approval for the scheme.

Kingfisher. Photo: Caroline Duncan

Improvements to the river have been rewarded by increases in the presence of key protected species. Kingfishers are sighted regularly along the lower Crane. They create their nests by driving tunnels into the banks, digging them by repeatedly flying into the bank at speed, so are able to nest in vertical riverbanks. Steep, penetrable earth banks are almost impossible to find in a heavily engineered urban river, so the group has helped to build two artificial nesting banks. These have been very successful; kingfishers have been using them to produce two or more broods each year.

The River Crane is one of the last places in London where you might see a water vole. This small mammal was once ubiquitous in Britain's rivers, but years of river engineering and consequent reductions in habitat have reduced their numbers. The local population, built up over years along the lower Crane and Duke of Northumberland's River, was devastated within weeks by what was believed to be a single, predatory mink. Local volunteers have been working to enhance water vole habitat through toe-board removal and river restoration – voles binge on Ranunculus blooms! They set up a mink monitoring system to help reduce the voles' risk of predation and they hope to release more water voles into the river corridor in 2023 to build on their existing fragile numbers and encourage them to re-populate their newly enhanced habitat.

Public access to the river and its open spaces is key to public engagement in wildlife promotion. The Friends of the River Crane

Little egret. Photo: Caroline Duncan

Environment have worked with developers and the local councils to create a network of high-quality pedestrian and cycle paths throughout the lower Crane corridor. This provides mental and physical health benefits as well as green transport options. Crane Park hosts a Parkrun, as part of the worldwide Parkrun movement, in which some 150 local residents take part each week.

Twickenham Station provides a convenient access to the River Crane, but many visitors to the nearby Rugby Football Union Stadium – and even some local residents – don't realise that the river is here. The riverside path west, from which chub and roach can regularly be seen in the water below, leads to Twickenham Junction Rough, a linear space opened to the public in 2018 after over a century as railway land and market gardens. Beyond, an eel pass and the river-naturalisation field trial can be viewed from Craneford Recreation Ground.

Further along the path, in 2003, was the disused Mereway allotment site, one of a series of degraded and rather unloved open spaces that were accordingly proposed for housing development. However, many local people recognised the wildlife value and potential as community resources of these sites. That was the impetus for the formation of the Friends of the River Crane Environment group, and they successfully put forward to the Public Inquiry an alternative vision of environmentally enhanced and well-used public open spaces.

One of the group's first actions was to install a carved bench in the formerly threatened space. This "Fox" bench is still in place and has come to represent the space, now re-named as Mereway Nature Park. In the intervening years, the Friends, who are all volunteers, have installed seventeen further themed benches up and down the corridor, often in spaces which they have helped to enhance, and as a symbol of community and

Fox bench in Mereway Nature Park. Photo: FORCE

Operation Centaur. Photo: FORCE

environmental value and care.

Continuing west, the sounds of children playing in Kneller Gardens are eclipsed by birdsong in Crane Park, the ambient level of which is testament to the wide range of birdlife here. In addition to the kingfishers already noted, little egrets and a wide range of aquatic birds may be seen in the river, and woodpeckers, jays, wrens, and many others on the banks. Red kites are regular visitors, kestrels and sparrowhawks are regularly spotted, and a tawny owl can be heard at night.

The community group have planted over a kilometre of hedgerow along a park fence line, and they now organise teams every year to deliver hedge laying and management along the entire length on a five-year cycle. They helped to build a line of nine wetland scrapes along this hedge line, taking advantage of the fact that these areas were flooding regularly, to turn this problem into a habitat feature. These works have created a new linear habitat for bird nesting and a corridor for small mammals and amphibians to move along safely.

They have helped to create several new meadows and work with the shire horses of 'Operation Centaur' to cut these, which enhances their floral and invertebrate value. The horses ensure that the ground is not compressed, as their hooves tend to open up the soil; they operate in confined areas, and people love to work with them. Volunteers rake up the arisings following these twice-yearly hay cuts, and this helps to reduce the nutrients in the soil and encourage more wildflowers. They pile the grass in habitat mounds along the river edge for use by grass snakes and these have been seen swimming in the river in search of prey. Summer invertebrate surveys have revealed that rare red-list beetles are now living in these meadows.

In 2014, the Friends group started their first major Citizen Science project, known as "Citizen Crane". Working alongside London Zoo (ZSL), and with support from Thames Water and the Environment Agency, they set up a network of around sixty volunteers to monitor the river at twelve locations every month, and this has

River restoration trial on the River Crane.
Photo: Steve Marshall / Wild Future

continued ever since. Kick-sampling is used to collect river invertebrates, and these are identified and counted to provide a proxy for water quality and habitat value. Water samples are sent to a Thames Water laboratory to assess them for key pollution indicators. This work has allowed the team to develop a sophisticated understanding of the river ecosystem and helped to identify many pollution issues and target remediation measures.

Partly as a result of this Citizen Crane initiative, in 2020, Thames Water selected the River Crane as the UK's first urban "Smarter Water Catchment". This is a ten-year programme of investment and engagement to see how an urban river system functions and can best be enhanced for environmental and community benefit. The Smarter Water Catchment programme is a major and natural extension of the work FORCE started back with their first volunteer event in the summer of 2003. Their vision for 2030 is for well-functioning corridors of open spaces, linking the River Thames with the Chilterns, teeming with wildlife, and providing health, education, training, and employment opportunities for many of the 650,000 people who live and work in the catchment area.

The Friends group now have the backing of the five local authorities through which the River Crane flows, and access to funding and high-level technical expertise, alongside over fifty other community groups that share their desire to make this happen. With this support they look forward to the River Crane continuing to improve as a community and environmental asset for the people of West London.

For further information about the Crane Valley and the community groups that help look after it:

www.force.org.uk

www.cranevalley.org.uk

www.cvcic.org.uk

www.tcv.org.uk/london

www.operationcentaur.com

www.habitatsandheritage.org.uk

www.lgoal.org

River Crane. Photo: Crane Valley Partnership

Great crested grebes at London Wetland Centre. Photo: LWC

Darlands Lake. Photo: Dudley Miles

DARLANDS NATURE RESERVE, TOTTERIDGE

Roger Tichborne

The Darlands Nature Reserve is one of the hidden gems of North West London. The reserve sits in the Totteridge Valley between the villages of Totteridge and Mill Hill in the London Borough of Barnet. It comprises a lake, woodlands, and several trails with spectacular views as you walk up from the valley by the lake and Folly Brook, towards Totteridge Lane, which is on the ridge of the hill.

The site was once part of Copped Hall, an estate dating from the sixteenth century. From 1780 it was occupied by William Manning MP. His son, Cardinal Manning, was born there. Darlands Lake was created as an ornamental lake by damming Folly Brook, reputedly planned by William Manning's wife, Mary, with advice from Humphry Repton, a well-known landscape gardener of the time. Repton also designed the Woburn estate and Russell Square for the Duke of Bedford and originally designed the grounds of Kenwood. Other commissions included Cassiobury in Watford and Wanstead Park.

Darlands was designated as a nature reserve in 1982 and is owned by Barnet Council. In 2007, some restoration work was done around the lake, with repairs to the dam, however the reserve was not well tended. Luckily, in 2017 a conservation trust was set up and they have actively started to do much needed maintenance. Whilst the reserve is once again looking well cared for, there is still vital repair work to be done on the lake. It has silted up over the years, making it quite shallow – shallow enough in fact to completely dry out during the summer 2022 drought. This presents a problem for the local wildlife as it is an important source of water for many species. The trust has launched an appeal to fund these important works and to preserve this important natural resource.

The lake has extensive reed beds, which provide a home for many species of insects and spiders, the reserve also includes woodlands, which are an ideal habitat for a diverse range of butterflies and breeding birds. It provides a home for adders, slow worms, grass snakes, amphibians, fungi, and invertebrates.

When walking by the lake, if you look carefully, you may see a bank vole looking up at you, or a weasel crossing your path. A total of eighteen different mammals can be seen around the reserve, including stoats, foxes and muntjac deer.

The lake and woods are a haven for birds, such as the reed bunting, hobby, sparrowhawk, jackdaw, stock dove, mandarin duck, and a variety of common waterfowl. In the spring, it is generally the first place you will hear a cuckoo in the London Borough of Barnet. It is an important stop-off point for migratory birds, who draw a large audience of local bird watchers. There are guided walks, and highlights include such birds as Mistle Thrushes, Red Kite and Spotted Flycatchers. In total, local ornithologists have logged over a hundred different species of bird in the valley.

In addition to the birds, you will encounter all manner of wonderful wildlife on a visit, including those that might give you a bit of a fright. One of the most impressive is the wasp spider. The females are large, colourful spiders, up to 17mm in length; males are smaller and less distinctive to help avoid predation by hungry females. They are recent arrivals to the UK from the continent and have slowly spread over the south of England. Putting the scary appearance aside, this is a magnificent spider. It builds large orb webs in grassland and heathland and attaches its silk egg-sacs to the grasses. The web has a wide white zig-zag strip running down the middle, known as a 'stabilimentum', the function of which is unclear. Mating is a dangerous game for males; they wait at the edge of the web until the female has moulted into a mature form, then take advantage of her jaws being soft and rush in to mate. However, many males still get eaten during this time.

Another creature which might initially give you a bit of a scare, is the hornet; mention them and one always imagines a large and terrifying insect. There's little doubt that the European hornet (*Vespa Crabro),* is a rather fearsome-looking insect. This ferocious exterior betrays a species that is rarely aggressive. Unlike their infamous relatives, hornets are unlikely to disrupt your picnic. Their size, (between 2-3 cm for workers

Wasp spider. Photo: Samuel Levy

European hornet. Photo: Samuel Levey

and males, and 3-4 cm for queens), and riotous buzz can still make them an intimidating proposition. They are our largest and most impressive wasp species, displaying the very highest level of organisation of animal sociality and their average size being more than double that of our more familiar common wasp.

The European hornet is a docile creature, avoiding conflict and rarely displaying any form of aggression unless the nest is approached or the colony is threatened. If you leave them alone, they will leave you alone in return. Once you realise that they wish you no harm, enjoy their beauty and magnificence.

Less familiar to general audiences are insects such as rose chafers, and they are often overlooked in discussions of wildlife. When a closer look is taken, they are fascinating subjects. The upper surfaces are an iridescent emerald green and bronze colour. The underside is a bronze colour. There are ragged white marks running widthways across the wing casings which look like fine cracks. Rose chafers are also surprisingly furry; the wing casings which look very smooth and shiny are actually covered in tiny hairs. Rose chafers are usually seen on warm sunny days feeding on pollen and nectar. Their favoured plant, as their name suggests, is the rose. Across Darlands, there are many wild roses growing, presumably remnants from the days when the site housed ornamental gardens.

The meadow grasshopper is mainly a resident of damp, unimproved pastures and meadows. Grasshoppers go through a series of moults, from wingless nymphs to winged adults, shedding their exoskeletons as they grow. Nymphs are present from April onwards, maturing into adults in June, who feed on plants and grass. Adult males can be seen displaying to females by rubbing their legs against their wings to create a 'song' – in the

Rose chafer beetle. Photo: Samuel Levey

Meadow Grasshopper. Photo: Samuel Levy

case of the meadow grasshopper, this is a regular 'rrrr' sound. After mating, the eggs are laid in the soil in a pod, ready to hatch the following spring. The Darlands reserve is alive with the sound of these wonderful insects on warm summer evenings

Non-native species are regularly found setting up home in the reserve, such as the green parakeets which are hard to ignore. Another recent addition is the Willow Emerald Damselfly. Just a decade ago, the Willow Emerald Damselfly had only been reliably recorded in the UK on two occasions, in 1979 and 1992. In recent years, however, the Willow Emerald has spread rapidly across the Southeast of England, gaining footholds in new counties on a yearly basis. Now, they are regularly seen around Darlands. They are most commonly spotted in and around the reed beds.

Luckily, there are still many native species to be seen, which haven't been pushed out by non-native insects, including a whole host of interesting butterflies and moths to see at the Darlands Nature Reserve. Although relatively common, a favourite is the easily recognisable Peacock butterfly, with its brownish-red wings, each with a single, large peacock-feather-like eyespot that is designed to scare predators. It rests with its wings closed, showing the almost black, well-camouflaged underside. It is one of the most common garden butterflies, found throughout lowland England and Wales.

Willow Emerald Damselfly. Photo: Samuel Levy

In May, after mating, females lay their eggs in batches of up to five hundred. After a week or two, the caterpillars hatch and spin a communal web in which they live and feed. As they grow, the caterpillars increasingly live in the open. They pupate alone, and adults emerge from July, which is the best time to see them at Darlands. Their main priority is to feed-up before the winter, when they hibernate in dark crevices, sheds, and tree holes. Adults will emerge again in spring to mate and breed.

Peacock caterpillars are black, covered with short spines and speckled with white spots. They are usually found on stinging nettles, of which there are plenty around Darlands.

The Darlands Nature Reserve is a perennial place for a visit. The 32 hectares (80 acres) of woodlands, wetlands, and grasslands boast some wonderful rural walks with spectacular views across the valley. One of the most popular walks starts at Burtonhole Lane, near the 240 Bus stop in Mill Hill, walking to the lake, and then up the hill to Totteridge Lane, emerging by the Orange Tree Pub and the 251 bus stop.

In the spring, you will see migratory birds heading northwards and the butterflies emerging from hibernation. In the summer, you will see all manner of flora and fauna, and in the autumn, there are amazing colours to view as the leaves change colour, as well as the sight of the migratory birds heading south.

The winter snow sees some beautiful and picturesque landscapes but wear sturdy footwear as the paths can get very muddy. Make sure to bring a camera and some binoculars to get the very best from your visit.

A favourite time to walk around Darlands is as the sun is rising or as the sun is setting. There is always a lot of activity as the birds and other animals start their day. You are more likely to see some of the shyer species that are none too keen on company. You may get the added bonus of a spectacular sunrise or sunset!

Bridge Across Folly Brook. Photo: Martin Addison

Late summer sunrise over the Rick Pond in Home Park. Photo: Sue Lindenberg

Dukes Meadows. Photo: Irid Escent

DUKES MEADOWS, CHISWICK

Ian Alexander

The low-lying land in the southern part of Chiswick, in a large bend of the river Thames, was protected from development by frequent flooding. As late as 1902, the area consisted of marsh, meadows, and orchards. In 1923, the ninth Duke of Devonshire sold the land to Chiswick Urban District Council. The council paid for the purchase by digging gravel from the site until 1937; the gravel pits have since been filled in.

Parts of the 170-acre site now serve as playing fields, providing access to nature in the form of fresh air and outdoor exercise for many groups of people. To the west of the railway are Chiswick Rugby Football Club and Dukes Meadows Golf, Tennis, and Ski; the riverside strip remains as parkland. To the east of the railway are the Virgin Active sports centre, and the King's House sports ground, with an open area that runs down to the river. Allotments, yet another way of getting back to nature by growing your own food, occupy a strip near the river, and a rectangle beside the Farmers' Market.

The areas of parkland became somewhat rundown and neglected in the late twentieth century and attracted fly-tippers. From 2000, local people came together and formed the Dukes Meadows Trust with the goal of improving the area. They raised

The renovated play area at Dukes Meadows. Photo: Kathleen Healy

Medlar tree in fruit. Photo: Ian Alexander

money to renovate the play areas, including the disused paddling pools. They have since transformed the area into a popular space for families in the summer with a modern adventure play area, new paddling pool and café.

Nearer the river, the once bare area of species-poor grass is flourishing as wildflower meadows, an orchard with many species of fruit tree, some of them provided by Abundance London, and hedgerows. It's fun visiting the orchard in autumn to see all the different kinds of fruit, some of them really quite unfamiliar, like medlars which are similar to apples. They are only edible when "bletted", that is, kept until wintertime when they go brown inside and becomes deliciously squashy.

These well-chosen plantings have provided habitats for fungi, with attractive

The pretty Hare's Foot Inkcap fungi. Photo: Ian Alexander

The Food Market Chiswick. Photo: Kathleen Healy

species like the egghead mottlegill, the hare's foot inkcap, and the blistered cup on the wood-chip mulch scattered under the fruit trees. The mottlegill is a tiny mushroom, with an egg-domed cap, slender stem, and a mottled pattern; it can appear in large numbers, forming an impressive troop.

The Inkcap dissolves into a black inky mess when it gets old, but when fresh its fruiting bodies look like tiny, furry, rabbit feet. The blistered cup resembles a warty selection of goblins' ears that have unaccountably popped out of the ground before Hallowe'en. They're spore-shooter fungi, which form strange tongues, discs, and cups instead of mushrooms.

Also flourishing is the Chiswick Farmers' Market, held every Sunday in the car park by the old Dukes Meadows farmhouse. Among its delights are fresh bread, cakes, cheeses, apples, delicatessen, sushi, cider, meat and vegetables. Its aim is to bring townspeople into direct contact with those who grow fruit and vegetables, raise animals, or otherwise create wonderful food: back to nature in a practical way. Some of the goods are undeniably luxuries, but many are fantastic value, fresh to a point that supermarkets struggle to match, with the chance of a conversation with people who really know about what they are selling.

They organise special events too on Sundays, such as an Easter Treasure Hunt, a Birds of Prey display, Punch & Judy shows and donkey rides during the school summer holidays.

For more info:
www.abundancelondon.com
www.dukesmeadowstrust.org
www.thefoodmarketchiswick.com

Spanish delicatessan. Photo: Ian Alexander

Squirrel in Richmond Park. Photo: Tim Felce

"WILDNESS IS THE PRESERVATION OF
THE WORLD."

– Henry David Thoreau

Mandarin duck in Kew Gardens. Photo: James Yates

Studying pond life from the boardwalk

GUNNERSBURY TRIANGLE

Ian Alexander

The land to the north of Chiswick High Road survived as countryside into the nineteenth century, rich with orchards. The growth of London spurred the development of suburban railways, and by 1877 the District Railway and the London and South Western Railway between them had built a triangle of three gently-curving lines, linking tracks to Hammersmith, Richmond, and Acton.

Gunnersbury Triangle became a gravel quarry and then railwaymen's allotment gardens. It was abandoned in the mid-twentieth century, and nature took over. In what biologists call a succession, grasses colonised bare ground, brambles sprang up, birch and cherry saplings grew from seed, with willows rooting in the wetter places.

George Monbiot suggested in his controversial book *Feral: Rewilding the Land, Sea, and Human Life* that all you need to do to make a nature reserve is to leave nature to do its own thing (as Gunnersbury Triangle once did). But in a small urban reserve, you have to balance nature conservation against safe public access and the needs of education. If a tree half-falls and lodges precariously where people will walk under it, you can't just leave it. Similarly, if children are to study pond life, you need something safe that they can sit on next to the water, like a boardwalk.

With the current trend for rewilding you may wish to create a wildflower meadow to encourage biodiversity, but to maintain its wild state you will need to mow it every year or the succession to forest will take over. If you have a site where you can keep animals safely, as at the London Wetland Centre in Barnes, you can use sheep or cattle to graze the meadow. They nip off any new shoots, preventing trees from colonising the area. If not, you have to simulate the grazing action with regular cutting. This can be done with traditional tools such as scythes, giving townspeople the opportunity to learn some old country skills.

In 1981, a property developer planned to cover Gunnersbury Triangle with industrial units. In response, local people formed the Chiswick Wildlife Group, campaigning to save it. That same year, the London Wildlife Trust was formed, and it took up the challenge. In 1983, the development went to a public inquiry. For the first time for any urban site in Britain, the inquiry ruled that the Triangle should be kept for nature. Professor David Goode, then the Greater London Council's ecologist, commented that it had none of the traditional attributes of a place worth preserving, like being the roost of rare horseshoe bats, but its woodland was "the only genuinely wild place for miles around, and it was greatly cherished by local people."

Stag beetles from the root of a pear tree

Since 1985, Gunnersbury Triangle has been managed as a local nature reserve by London Wildlife Trust. I first heard of it around 1990, when the company I worked for took out corporate membership, and everyone was given a copy of the Wildlife Trust magazine. I remember my first reaction: *What, there's wildlife in London!* I knew the ducks on the Round Pond in Kensington Gardens, and squirrels dodging the dogs to run up the trees, but that was about it. The magazine was a revelation.

Most of the work in Gunnersbury Triangle is done by volunteers. I've been a volunteer there since 2013, developing skills from tree-pruning to hedge-laying, not to mention digging ditches, building boardwalks, and repairing nest boxes. I've discovered just how much wildlife there can be in a few hectares, encountering everything from handsome urban foxes in broad daylight to monstrous-looking but quite harmless stag beetles with great curved jaws.

The marvellous *Field Guide to the Dragonflies of Britain and Europe* noted an odd thing: there is plenty of suitable habitat in Britain for the willow emerald damselfly, but it had not been seen here. In 2015, as if by magic, this elegantly slim insect, shimmering in iridescent green like a Hollywood belle at the Oscars, arrived in Gunnersbury Triangle.

Females lay their eggs inside willow twigs, cutting little slits in the bark. The willow twigs have to be over freshwater, so the hatching damselfly nymphs can fall into the water and feed on tiny pond animals. We regularly cut the willow by the pond so the area stays light and airy for pond life, but we always leave some twiggy shoots for the damselflies.

Another speciality of the

The dazzling Willow Emerald Damselfly

A slow worm mother and young

reserve is the slow worm – neither a worm nor a snake, but a legless lizard. The reserve manager insisted that if we kept "reptile corridors" open with carpet squares to act as "refugia" (warm places safe from predators), the slow worms would come. We cleared the brambles and waited.

A few years later, I gingerly lifted one of the carpet squares, and was rewarded with the astonishing sight of a smooth scaly mother slow worm and her young. As they slithered away, I hastily snapped a blurry photo, quickly putting the cover down again, concerned not to scare them off.

Since then, we've made several reptile corridors in quiet corners. The slow worms surely arrived from the adjacent railway, whose embankments form a network of unofficial nature reserves all over the city.

If you have a garden that backs onto a wildlife-friendly area, you might try creating a refuge for some of London's less often seen residents, like slow worms or hedgehogs. If you have a small space, even a balcony, you could put up a bee-house, nestbox, or bird-feeder to help wildlife thrive.

Bits of railway archæology still surface in the Triangle from time to time as we clear brambles. A huge old apple tree is surely a survivor from the railway gardens which were created by railway workers. The raspberry canes and redcurrant bushes dotted about the reserve are probably descendants of plants in those gardens.

Ancient apple tree in fruit

An ancient apple tree, leaning almost horizontally over a path, is probably a survivor of a railwayman's garden on the site.

To visit Gunnersbury Triangle, close to Chiswick Park Station::
https://www.wildlondon.org.uk/nature-reserves/gunnersbury-triangle

All photos courtesy of Ian Alexander

Late spring sunrise over the Boating Pond in Bushy Park. Photo: Sue Lindenberg

"TO LOVE A PLACE IS NOT ENOUGH. WE MUST FIND WAYS TO HEAL IT."

– Robin Wall Kimmerer

Red deer and western jackdaw in Richmond Park. Photo: James Yates

Autumn Trees. Photo David Wilson

HAMPSTEAD HEATH

David Templer

Even if you are a city-dweller, you may well be deeply aware of the natural world around you. However, there is a difference between believing that cities should contain natural places, such as parks, and recognising that the world is in fact a large natural place, containing towns.

Hampstead Heath of course is far from being just a 'park': with its large open spaces, it is the result of aristocratic traditions combining with the emerging values of a new middle class, years before climate change focused us on the necessity of saving and maintaining wild places.

With 30 lakes and ponds, and numerous habitats including areas of heathland, scrubland, woodland and meadows, the Heath is home to many common species including moles, hedgehogs and muntjac deer, according to a survey in September 2020. It also supports 200 types of spider and 9 kinds of bat..

Heath Hands, a registered charity, works in conjunction with English Heritage and The City of London Corporation to manage 350 acres of wild Heathland heather and gorse, along with its famous wetlands and its peaceful woodland glades. Rich wildflower meadows have been created, supporting 650 kinds of wildflowers and plants, while trees like willow and hawthorn provide habitats for insects and birds.

Winged visitors to the Heath in summer include herons, swallows, and swifts, and a large variety of other birds from spotted flycatchers to doves. Autumn visitors include the whinchat and the wheatear; redwings and siskins have also been spotted there in the winter months.

Bright green ring-necked parakeets nest on the Heath, making it one of the homes to the many thousands now in London. They are threatening to outnumber the town's pigeons, and, flying in fast-moving squadrons, are 'well

Bluebells on the Heath. Photo: Cristiane Teston

Parakeet outside its nest. Photo: James Ó Nuanáin

able to outmanoeuvre birds in the feeding frenzy at bird tables' (Nick Hunt, the *Guardian*, 2019). All these species are free to interact naturally with one another on the Heath, as well as with humans, providing a place where people can pick sloes, for gin, and bullaces, for jam, while blackberries proliferate seasonally.

The woodlands are full of butterflies in the summer (27 different species): brimstones, fritillaries, peacocks and orange tips may be seen there. Eighteen kinds of damselfly and dragonfly may be found as well from spring and around early June at various ponds. Four hundred species of moth are found there, different varieties of which can be encountered all year long.

Scrubland, a kind of transitional state between grass and woods, and is a valuable habitat for wildlife providing seeds, fruits, shelter and nest sites for invertebrates, birds, and mammals. It offers living space for different types of flowering plant, as well as many wild animals, from fox and deer, to rabbits, mice and the hawks which prey on them, and is actively managed on the Heath so as to maintain its distribution, stop it encroaching into other habitats, and ensure that a crucial refuge for wildlife is conserved.

While it is now a public area, Hampstead Heath originally included the private garden of Kenwood House. The house was home to a Lord Mansfield up until the 18th century, and Victorian developers could not decide what to do with it. Due partly to a long-running property dispute in the 19th century, Lord Mansfield's leafy, unspoiled world has become an escape from the capital's polluted streets. The legal case made it as far as the House of Lords, when it was resolved that the space should be left to Londoners in an Act of Parliament (1871). This opened with the declaration that "it would be of great advantage to the inhabitants of the Metropolis if the Heath were always kept unenclosed and unbuilt on in its natural aspect and state being as far as may be preserved…"

Local liberals of the time, pressing for the preservation of Heathland, put up a long fight to have a wild open space at the heart of their city, leading to the establishment of the Hampstead Heath Protection Fund Committee in 1866 (now the Hampstead Heath Society). The whole site was acquired by the Metropolitan Board of Works in

1875, and has been managed successively by The London County Council, The Greater London Council, Camden Council and the City of London Corporation. In 1927, Edward Cecil Guinness (Lord Iveagh) gifted Kenwood House with its collection of art and its Robert Adam Library, making up the Iveagh Bequest.

As you walk downhill over different soils through Kenwood (originally Caen Wood) and North Wood today, you move beneath a type of canopy of trees that is uncommon nationally and very scarce in Greater London. Fine-leaved grasses and sorrel gradually give way to lusher broad-leaved grasses. Small areas of acid grassland are of particular note, with plants like heath bedstraw, oval sedge and tormentil. As you may well know, acid grassland and meadowland are both among the UK's fastest-disappearing habitats.

Generally, on Hampstead Heath, any dead wood is left lying where it falls, and old dead trees are left standing for as long as it is safe to do so. Dying wood actually offers a vital habitat for a range of species, including stag beetles and the Heath's eight hundred kinds of fungi, which in their turn help invertebrates that live on old or dead trees. These include the rare bracket fungus *Ganoderma lucidum*.

Other rare plants include broad-leaved helleborine and lady fern (woodland); cowslip, black knapweed, devil's-bit scabious and pignut (grassland); marsh marigold, yellow iris and water mint (wetland). Heath Hands point out that the Heath protects many ancient hedgerows, including important ones on Parliament Hill mentioned in the Domesday book. The Heath also hosts many endangered species of plant and moss, as well as specialist invertebrates.

The 790 acres of Hampstead Heath have distinct purposes and identities. There are Parliament Hill Fields, with its athletics track, its open-air Lido, its paddling pool and its cricket club; there is Highgate Golf Course; the Heath Extension, where much of Hampstead Garden Suburb now stands, and Hampstead Ponds, home to wild water

Kenwood House lawns. Photo: Alastairmck

Egyptian goose goslings. Photo: Garry Knight

swimmers all year.

Wetland habitats are as important for the conservation of nature as they are for recreation. In addition to a variety of waterfowl, ponds on Hampstead Heath support many species of dragonfly, with the frogs, toads, and newts which are prey to grass snakes (the longest British snake) making up a thriving population of snakes that is the closest one to Central London. Commonly sighted water birds include moorhens, gulls, coots, swans, and of course mandarin ducks.

Just as grass snakes depend on wetland amphibians and plants for food, submerged and partly-submerged aquatic plants support both amphibians and insects, while recent planting and the creation of new wetland areas further aid biodiversity. The City of London Corporation reports an increase in sightings of snakes around the bird sanctuary pond since its programme started in 2009.

Volunteers work with Heath Rangers to improve water quality and control invasive plant species like Himalayan balsam, which can grow to a great size, competing with other wetland and woodland plants.

In addition to the wildlife, domesticated animals and people make full use of the Heath. Horses still get exercised on the Heath today (the Royal Horse Artillery regiment uses it, as do many private owners). Large and small dogs streak about off their leashes there, and footballers have their regular (unmarked) pitches, as well as baseball players and kite-flyers, making use of wind that is almost always blowing 320 feet above London.

Model boats also still sail on Whitestone Pond, (although carriages are no longer driven into its waters to clean off mud), an annual 'affordable' art fair pops up

Heron hunting on the ponds. Photo: Neville Young

Model Boating Pond. Photo: Ricardalovesmonuments

in May, filming happens regularly, (*Notting Hill* was partly filmed there in 1999), as well as much photography. Concerts are arranged each summer among the rhododendrons in the four meadows around Kenwood House (often making use of the little concert shell at the bottom of a hill beside an ornamental lake.)

Another distinct area is The Vale of Health, visited by the poets Byron, Keats and Shelley, inhabited by novelist D.H Lawrence, newspaper founder and editor Lord Northcliffe, and critic Leigh Hunt. It is possibly the closest you can get to living in an English village while being in the heart of London. The sandy slopes of the Vale of Health also host London's oldest known population of purse web spiders.

The view over the city toward the Houses of Parliament, six miles away from Parliament Hill (where Roundheads assembled in the English Civil War) is one of a few that is protected by an Act of Parliament. A key ley line lies between Parliament Hill and the White Hill in the Tower of London, the line in which the sun rises on Midsummer's Day.

The Heath's paths are, in part, an extension of the work of the great landscape gardener Humphry Repton, who worked on the area around Kenwood House, with a close eye on its natural features.

Ever since it was made into a public space, Londoners frequently journeyed to the Heath for recreation or amusement. As the *Hampstead and Highgate Express* recorded in 1880: "On Easter Monday there were not far short of 80,000 visitors to Hampstead Heath." This has only increased over the last century, with up to fifteen million visitors recorded in 2021. With views from one of the highest points in London, its long sandy paths through woods, and its iconic ponds, the numbers are hardly surprising.

Kenwood Woods. Photo: London Less Travelled

Kew Gardens greenhouse. Photo: James Yates

KEW GARDENS

Susanne Masters

All seems tame at the Royal Botanic Gardens at Kew. Flowerbeds are immaculate; tidily weeded, with crisp edges, and plants carefully pruned. This garden is captive within the capital city's sprawl. Yet wildness is written through its fabric with local wildlife joining in.

In the Mediterranean garden, spikes of pale-yellow flowers punch through a glossy patch of leaves. The flowers are Ivy broomrape (*Orobanche hederae*), the leaves ivy (*Helix hedera*). When ivy broomrape seeds germinate they seek ivy roots. Puncturing them allows ivy broomrape to be a plant that doesn't make leaves; it meets all its needs for water, carbohydrates, and nutrients by taking them from the ivy. We don't know how this parasitic relationship began. Perhaps a gardener scattered seed near ivy in hope of growing ivy broomrape, or perhaps seeds in the soil took advantage of a gardener's offering of ivy.

Summertime, with a bird's eye view of tree canopy from Kew's treetop walkway, you can see bees making use of abundant pollen and nectar from flowering trees. Bees have red knees in May when they have been collecting pollen from horse chestnuts (*Aesculus hippocastanum*). Later in June, they'll return to harvest from tassels of flowers on sweet chestnuts (*Castanea sativa*). Winter is not a time of such floral abundance, but follow the rhododendron walk and you may catch the sharp call and dainty sight of goldcrests (*Regulus regulus*), the UK's smallest resident bird. Evergreen trees host plenty of insects for these insect-eating birds to forage in cold months of the year.

Kew isn't just a space for local wildlife within Greater London's urban area; it sustains rare living examples of wildlife from distant places and distant times and offers prospects for restoring wildlife in the UK and around the world.

Even as far back as the 16th century there were private

Brown Hawker. Photo: James Yates

gardens at Kew. A pivotal moment that ushered Kew Gardens into global significance was in 1759 when Princess Augusta established a collection of exotic plants over nine-acres. Within ten years there were at least 3400 plant species growing on the site, more than double the number of plant species considered native to Britain. In 1840, the transfer of Kew Gardens from the Crown to the government, and the subsequent opening of them to the public, marked a shift in ethos that enabled the gardens to extend their benefits to more people. Four centuries of gardening, and the surrounding growth of brick-built homes and traffic-laden streets, give a veneer of domestication. Yet spending time at Kew Gardens quickly brings the sensations of being in other wild places.

Within the sharp angles of the Princess of Wales Conservatory there are ten different climatic zones. In its hot steamy centre you'll take off coats and sweaters because the temperature and humidity that allows plants like the Titan arum (*Amorphophallus titanum*) to thrive is too hot for people wearing cold weather clothing. When Kew's Titan arum is in the news for flowering it isn't just the visual spectacle of a column over two metres tall formed of thousands of tiny flowers that draws crowds. Growing wild in rainforests on limestone hills on the island of Sumatra, Indonesia, Titan arum's flowers attract pollinators by releasing the stench of rotting flesh. Flowers that stink, rather than waft fragrance, offer novelty value and this has made the plant one of the most popular visitor attractions to the Gardens. Since 1889, the first time a Titan arum flowered outside of Indonesia, this olfactory and visual spectacle has been one of the ways that Kew showcases wildlife from around the world.

Sections for cooler zoned plants are built into the conservatory design as buffers between its hot heart and English weather outside. Alongside the tropical pool where Amazon waterlily (*Victoria amazonica*) grows is a room filled with carnivorous plants. One of which is Venus flytrap (*Dionaea muscipula*), notable as a plant that can count numbers and measure time. It catches insects by rapidly closing pads

Titan arum at Kew. Photo: Patche99z

Venus flytraps at Kew. Photo: Wolfgang Stuppy

fringed with interlocking bristles. Further closing squashes the insect, which is then digested with enzymes. The plant's traps are triggered to shut when small hairs on the pads are disturbed twice within 20 seconds.

Both Titan arum and Venus flytrap are at risk of extinction in their homelands. In Sumatra, timber harvesting and the conversion of forest to oil palm plantations, has changed and removed the habitat Titan arum grows in. Collection of Venus flytraps for horticultural trade has reduced wild populations, and so has habitat loss. Their habitat of wet longleaf pine savanna in North Carolina, USA, has declined to only 3% of its former range due to agriculture and development. While insects supply Venus flytraps with nutrients that aren't readily available from the soil they grow in, these plants need sunlight in order to photosynthesise and produce carbohydrates for their energetic demands. Venus flytraps need frequent fires that remove shrubby undergrowth, allowing light to reach small plants. In the wild, longleaf pine savanna in lightning-prone territory has fires often enough to supress shrubby growth . At Kew, gardeners serve the role of fire-starting lightning bolts, by placing their Venus flytraps in well-lit positions.

Marianne North included Venus flytraps in her painting of North American carnivorous plants, alongside the California pitcher plant (*Darlingtonia californica*), and purple pitcher plant (*Sarracenia purpurea*). She used plants grown at Kew as her models, and you can see this painting in the Marianne North gallery at Kew. In the rock garden are purple pitcher plants, which were retrieved from Lower Hyde Heath in Wareham, Dorset. They had been introduced to a patch of bog and their success was crowding out local plants. Horticulturalists removed them from their wild escapade in Dorset and rehomed them at Kew.

Kew Gardens' boundary between cultivated and wild is permeable. Behind the public façade of beautiful gardens which often interact with displays of fine art, much work takes place to propagate rare species, with the hope not only of sustaining their existence in cultivation but also to reintroduce them back to their wild origins. When rare orchids flower they are pollinated and their seeds are sent to the Millennium Seed Bank Partnership for storage. To pollinate tiny orchids such as *Pleurothallis restrepioides*, horticulturalists use a strand of human hair as a fine-tipped tool to transfer pollinia from one individual plant to another.

Wood's cycad (*Encephalartos woodii*) is an individual resident at Kew that may never have its pollen turned into seeds. In 1895, on a botanical expedition in Ongoye Forest, KwaZulu-Natal, in South Africa, one stately cycad with buttressed and erect stems was seen. Botanists returned in 1903 and collected suckers from around the base of the plant that were sent to Durban Botanic Gardens, and to Kew. Further collections of suckers and main trunks in 1907 and 1916 removed the last stems. Despite hunts for more plants, in particular female plants, none have been found in the wild. So Wood's cycad exists only as clones of a male plant in a few botanic gardens including Kew. Ongoye Forest is now protected as a Nature Reserve, and it is possible that a female Wood's cycad could be found there that has been missed by previous surveys. There is also a chance that a Wood's cycad may, as documented in rare instances with other cycad species, spontaneously change sex.

Eastern Cape giant cycad - the oldest pot plant in the world. Photo: C T Johansson

Chinese Water Dragon. Photo: James Yates

Being collected in 1903 makes Wood's cycad sound old, but it is not the oldest plant at Kew Gardens. That title may be claimed by an Eastern Cape giant cycad (*Encephalartos altensteinii*) that arrived in 1775 after being sailed from South Africa to London, and then transported up the Thames on a barge. In old age, it has reclined and is supported by props bearing some of its weight.

Since Kew's large and diverse plant collections were first founded , there has been a shift in the flow of plants in botanical gardens. Initially they were a nexus to which exotic plants were brought. Environmental changes have impinged on wild habitats around the world. Botanical gardens can no longer be simply collections of biodiversity, although they offer a refuge for species from diverse habitats. Housing one of the largest Herbariums in the world, Kew's process of digitising its records provides botanists globally with a vast archive for study and discovery. With more than three hundred scientists involved in research and conservation at Kew Gardens, and fieldwork with international collaborations, their mission to protect plants and fungi is increasingly urgent.

Now named as a World Heritage site, the Gardens' collections must work as repositories within which species can be understood and sustained, and from which wild habitats can be restored. Kew Gardens' ordered beds are not just hospitable to local wildlife; they are portals to distant wild places.

Veteran oak tree at sunrise in Richmond Park. Photo: Amanda Boardman

"I THINK HAVING LAND AND NOT RUINING IT IS THE MOST BEAUTIFUL ART THAT ANYBODY COULD EVER WANT."

– Andy Warhol

Female kestrel with a caterpillar snack in flight in Bushy Park. Photo: Sue Lindenberg

The bird hide. Photo: London Wetland Centre

LONDON WETLAND CENTRE

Lisa Woodward

It is quite remarkable to think of the vision required to be able to stand in front of four disused concrete Victorian reservoirs and imagine them as a beautiful nature reserve. Without that vision, London Wetland Centre wouldn't exist today.

Sir Peter Scott, the founder of WWT, the Wildfowl & Wetlands Trust (and the son of renowned explorer Scott of the Antarctic), had long dreamt of creating an urban wetland. While sadly he did not live to see the creation of this site, it was by sharing his vision with the rest of his team at WWT that a beautiful wildlife haven right in the middle of the sprawling London suburbs was brought to life. WWT London opened to the public in the year 2000.

There is no doubt that this was a real community scheme. Local residents campaigned for the development, Thames Water provided the land, while Berkeley Homes provided the infrastructure and the main visitor centre building. It was a passion project for many, and plenty of those involved at the start still have a deep connection to the Centre to this day.

The foundations for WWT London were already there, with many interesting and notable birds regular visitors to the existing reservoirs. In 1995, the reservoirs were broken up, and 500,000 cubic metres of soil removed and remixed. Over the next five years, a staggering 300,000 water plants, 8,000 wildflowers, and 27,000 trees were planted by hand. Twenty-seven bridges, 600 metres of boardwalk, and 3.4 kilometres of pathways were added, alongside six bird-watching hides and 27 water control sluices.

At the time of its opening, London Wetland Centre was the largest man-made wetland in any capital city of the world, with a beautiful network of shallow pools and wetland meadows for birds, mammals, amphibians, reptiles and insects. Within two years, London

A family enjoying the park. Photo: LWC

Wetland Centre was awarded Site of Special Scientific Interest (SSSI) status, designated by Natural England because of the nationally important number of wintering shoveler and gadwall ducks. That status is something that the team today works hard to protect, actively managing and shaping the reserve to give the wildlife it attracts the best possible habitats.

More than twenty years on, the centre boasts an incredible 2,399 wildlife species. Cetti's warbler, reed buntings, shoveler, grebes, water vole and bittern can now be spotted. We are visited by rare birds such as pacific golden plovers, bluethroats and spotted crakes. David Attenborough opened the reserve in 2000, and has since referred to it as "an extra lung for London".

Because London Wetland Centre is part of the Wildfowl and Wetlands Trust, there is understandably a focus on the birds that can be seen here. And there is an impressive range, with more than three hundred different species attracting much valued regular birdwatching visitors. Some of the most popular attractions for these keen birders include a manmade sand martin bank, which has reached 98% occupancy; the much-loved bittern that return year after year; oystercatchers, who have fledged young for the first time this year; and a rare pectoral sandpiper that decided to stop off at the Centre bringing keen birdwatchers from across the country to try and spot it.

There are not just wild birds to be seen here as the Centre also has their own "living collection" – a carefully curated collection of birds and mammals that tell WWT's story. Included in this are two Asian-claw otters: Tod and Honey. They are a favourite among visitors, and their daily feeds are a highlight for so many. Tod loves to twist and spin in the water; he is never still. Honey is a calmer soul, and can be recognised by the white patch under her chin. They bring huge smiles to everyone who gets to see them.

Tod and Honey, the Centre otters. Photo: LWC

Great crested grebes. Photo: LWC

Across the rest of the site, rare dragonflies, such as the Northern Hawker, can also be seen. In the evening, the sky is full of bats, with Daubenton's swooping across the water. Grass snakes and slow worms can be spotted by the particularly observant. Marsh frogs sing out loudly across the centre. Even the excellent Leopard slug, which is as distinctive as its namesake, is a resident.

It was never really in doubt that this was a place where nature could flourish. However, this is also a place where people thrive. The link between nature and wellbeing is now well established. Research from 1972 to 1981 showed that hospital patients with a view of trees had shorter hospital stays and required less pain relief than those of a view with a brick wall. There is now a belief that "blue spaces" – an outdoor space predominantly

Marsh Frog, London Wetland Centre. Photo: Rakkhi Samarasekera

Children pond-dipping. Photo: LWC

filled with water – can lower stress and anxiety, while boosting people's mood and psychological wellbeing. Regular visitors, staff, members and volunteers will all tell you the same: London Wetland Centre is a sanctuary. No matter where you're from, or what you do, a walk around the reserve lifts you.

To that end, WWT is working with the Mental Health Foundation to trial Blue Prescriptions at the London Wetland Centre, a free programme for those suffering with low mood or poor mental health. The programme is designed to enable people to be active, take notice of wildlife and connect with other people in wetland settings, all to help people improve their mental health.

Wetlands are also vitally important in the fight against climate change. Urban wetlands can help reduce the air temperatures by five degrees; this will become increasingly significant as we continue to experience increased extreme temperatures. Wetlands are a fantastic resource against flooding, as they can store the excess water and slow down the flow of rain. They help to reduce carbon emissions, pulling carbon from the atmosphere and converting it into living plants and carbon-rich soil. Yet 90% of the wetlands in the UK have already disappeared, a combination of pollution, agriculture, urban development and water drainage. They are disappearing at three times the rate of forests.

This is one of the reasons why the centre has such a strong educational programme. The founder, Sir Peter Scott, was passionate about educating the next generation of conservationists and it is easy to see how connected to the environment young visitors are. The centre holds learning sessions for every age group, and welcomes up to five schools a day. It shouldn't be a privilege to access this kind of nature – which is why the centre runs programmes such as Generation Wild, a free education programme for schools in disadvantaged areas, using storytelling and adventure to share their message. It's why they open their doors – they are here to help visitors understand why wetlands are so important.

It's important that everyone understands their relationship with nature and how they can positively impact it. It's also important that nature is accessible to everyone. On a practical level, this means rather than walking through mud and fields, the Centre has proper paths throughout, suitable for wheelchairs, pushchairs and mobility scooters. They also work hard to make sure everyone feels comfortable here, and there is a team of one hundred-and-eighty valued volunteers who all contribute to this amazing welcome.

For a nature reserve, they are relatively young. But the site has matured hugely in the last twenty-two years, with the trees fully grown, well-established birds and wildlife, and a regular flow of visitors.

There have been many upgrades to the centre during that time. The otters now have a shiny enclosure fit for their lavish lifestyle. In 2019, the very popular Wild Walk was installed, which allows visitors to hop across logs, travel across a rope bridge, and practise their balance on the wooden beam. There are daily talks and exciting events, such as "Night Safaris" for families, who come along and use bat detectors to track bats, and toast marshmallows under the stars. It's impressive all that is achieved with the centre's 105 acres, and it's exciting to think how it will grow over the next twenty-two years.

Whatever the future brings, we can be sure that wildlife and visitors will be returning to the sanctuary of the London Wetland Centre for years to come.

The London Wetland Centre's sustainable gardens. Photo: LWC

London Wetland Centre at sunrise. Photo: LWC

The View to St Pauls, protected by act of Parliament. Photo: Diana Loch

RICHMOND PARK

Dr Vivienne Press

As both London's largest Royal Park and the largest urban park in Europe, covering an area of 2,500 acres, it is no surprise that Richmond Park holds such a special place in our society. It is a National Nature Reserve and a Site of Special Scientific Interest, holding both national and international importance for wildlife conservation. It's also the quietest place in London.

Richmond Park was established in its present form by King Charles I, who in 1637 enclosed the area on the hill above Richmond to form a hunting park and introduced herds of red and fallow deer. To this day, most of the 12 km wall he built around the edge of the Park remains, although some sections have been rebuilt and reinforced. Whilst the Kings allowed people to walk across some paths in the Park, it wasn't until legal action in 1758 by John Lewis, a local brewer, that the right of access for pedestrians at all times began to be established

Over the last nearly four hundred years, many woods have been planted mainly with oak, beech, sweet chestnut, and horse chestnut trees to provide food for the deer. There are now about 130,000 trees in the Park, including around 1,300 veterans. The first Lord Sidmouth, after his term in the early 19th century as Prime Minister, became a visionary Deputy Ranger of the Park. He not only planted three new woods and extended others, but most memorably, he also enclosed 42 acres of the Park to make a game reserve. This is now the magical Isabella Plantation, which was established in the 1950s and is famous for its azaleas and rhododendrons in the spring and colourful leaves in the autumn.

Azaleas, Isabella stream. Photo: Andrew Coleman

Red deer stag, making the browsing line.
Photo: Bartek Olszewski

In spite of these landscape changes, the essential character of the Park has not changed over the centuries; although it is now surrounded by the residential streets of Greater London, the varied landscape of hills, woodland gardens, and grasslands set among veteran trees abounds in wildlife. This incredible environment has been shaped through centuries of grazing by the herds of red and fallow deer. It is their feeding habits – eating all the leaves, twigs, and seedlings below 1.5 metres – which creates the 'browsing line' that gives the Park its very open look and feel.

There are currently around six hundred deer, attracting visitors from all over the world. If you spend time in the Park, you may be lucky enough to hear the primeval guttural roar of a stag on a crisp September morning heralding the start of the rut, the clatter of antlers either in playful jousting or a hind's gentle mew as she returns to feed her new-born calf concealed in the bracken. However, visitors must remember to give the deer space, even if they appear to be calm. Deer sitting ruminating (chewing the cud) is a vital part of their day, allowing a bolus of food to be coughed up and repeatedly chewed in order to extract the maximum amount of nutrients. Sitting still isn't an invitation to approach and, for both their safety and yours, it's recommended to keep at least fifty metres distance.

Whilst the deer are Richmond Park's most famous residents, it is home to a wide range of animals and plants, some rarely seen elsewhere in London. For example, both tawny and little owls live all around the Park. Although they're in small numbers, Richmond Park still probably has the largest population in Greater London.

Fungi can also be found in abundance around the Park. Saprotrophs – fungi that feed on

Little Owl. Photo: Paula Redmond

organic matter – are the best recyclers in the world and help the Park from being overrun by dead plant material. Some saprotrophic fungi choose specific hosts – the birch polypore only lives and feeds on birch, while others, such as turkey tail, are found on a wide variety of trees. Dyers mazegill will only grow on conifers, others only on deciduous trees. The oak polypore grows only on ancient oaks making it quite rare, but it does appear in Richmond Park. Beefsteak and chicken of the woods fungi cause red rot in the heartwood of oaks in the Park. These fungi remove the cellulose leaving the darker red lignin. The rare Cardinal click beetle, found in Richmond and Bushy Parks, develops in the red rotten heartwood of old oaks, and also feeds on the larvae of other invertebrates living in there.

All of this wildlife is dependent on the trees of Richmond Park, particularly the veteran trees that are hundreds of years old and incredibly ecologically valuable. The Park's veteran and ancient oaks are up to nine hundred years old and are the most common veteran tree here. Each can support up to 2,300 species of fungi, invertebrates, birds, bats, and other mammals. Hawthorn is the second most common veteran tree in the Park. They can live for four hundred years, growing slowly to a maximum height of 15m, and have an abundance of character. The branches twist and turn and are irregularly spaced, while the trunks of older trees can divide into several twisting parts. Like the oaks, they are invaluable for biodiversity; caterpillars of many moths, like the lappet, depend on the leaves for food and the red haws or fruits are popular with small mammals and birds, especially fieldfares, redwings, and thrushes. Even dormice like to eat the flowers.

Given their importance, it's not surprising that The Royal Parks, the charity that

Mushrooms. Photo: Kasia Ciesielska-Faber

The Royal Oak. Photo: Eric Baldauf

manages the Park, supported by the Friends of Richmond Park charity, strives to take diligent care of the trees. The Friends have recently funded wooden fences around many of the veterans, which protect the tree's main roots. Inside the fencing, bracken, bramble, and other vegetation grows quickly, providing a habitat for wildlife – and a further disincentive for people to enter it. The Friends also raised the funding for the 44 disease-resistant elms of the new Elm Walk, planted in 2018 by The Royal Parks, to help these magnificent trees thrive again after the devastating Dutch elm disease.

The Friends or Richmond Park has over 3,600 members. Over 300 members, as volunteers, actively support the Park with their time and expertise through a wide variety of Friends' programmes. This includes practical conservation work, the Adopt-an-Area litter-picking scheme, staffing the Visitor Centre, campaigning and producing information about the Park, running Discoverers for children, recording birds and butterfly numbers and fundraising for conservation projects, including by sales of their spectacular calendar, and other unique gifts and cards at the Visitor Centre and their online shop.

As part of The Friends' Tread Lightly Campaign, they produced the award-winning film 'Richmond Park National Nature Reserve' narrated by their Patron Sir David Attenborough, who says: "There are simple things we can all do to help protect the Park so that it will remain a very special lace for generations to come. Please love it like I do and Tread Lightly in Richmond Park". The actions he refers to are to take nothing away, leave nothing behind and to respect the wildlife.

Greater protection of its wildlife has been necessary in recent years, as Richmond Park is suffering badly from extreme weather events related to climate change. The last three years have seen periods of intense rainfall, heatwaves and near-drought conditions. High rainfall damaged anthills, while drought dried up ponds, affecting the water-life including amphibians like newts, and hardened the ground so that invertebrates struggled to burrow into it. Trees were especially impacted with both water logging and dry weather affecting their roots.

At the same time, surging visitor numbers throughout the Covid-19 lockdowns meant paths were damaged and widened by people walking on the path edges to 'socially distance' from each other, inadvertently trampling adjacent vegetation in the process. The resulting bare soil led to more surface runoff after heavy rain and more footpath erosion.

So, The Royal Parks have recently started a major programme to restore and upgrade paths throughout the Park and to combat the impact of both flooding and drought. Behind these actions is their very timely Biodiversity Framework 2020–2030, which sets out, in a clear and succinct way, the vision to conserve and enhance biodiversity. The three key objectives are to increase the resilience of biodiversity to climate change, to protect, conserve and enhance priority and characteristic habitats and species, and to provide sensitive and sustainable access to nature for all.

As part of The Queen's Green Canopy initiative, The Royal Parks, helped by funding from the Friends of Richmond Park, is creating a new woodland in Richmond Park. This will have climate-resilient trees and shrubs that will support an increasing biodiversity and will enhance and help protect this important National Nature Reserve, which provides vital green space on the edge of the capital.

Richmond Park is open to the public every day and enjoyed by millions of visitors throughout the year. If you are looking to escape the city and enjoy peace, beauty and wildlife, there is hardly a better place to do it.

For more information about Richmond Park and the work of the Friends of Richmond Park: www.frp.org.uk.

With thanks to Janet Bostock (fungi and conservation volunteers), Christopher Hedley (trees) and Roger Hillyer (Chair, Friends of Richmond Park).

Woodland stream. Photo: Amanda Boardman

Frosty sunrise by the veteran oaks. Photo: Amanda Boardman

"TIME SPENT AMONGST TREES IS NEVER WASTED TIME."

– Katrina Mayer

Red Deer Stag late summer Bushy Park. Photo: Sue Lindenberg

Serotine bat. Photo: Hugh Clark, Bat Conservation Trust

RIVERBANKS OF THE THAMES

Philip Briggs

The River Thames in West London has many areas of excellent bat habitat alongside it. Except for the more intensively urbanised and brightly lit areas, virtually any green space or stretch of riverbank along the Thames will have at least some bat interest, and several are highly important sites for a wide range of species. This is because wetland habitats support high levels of insects, which are the main prey of British bats, and riverbanks have the added importance of providing wildlife corridors which bats will "commute" along when moving between their roosts and foraging areas.

Bats are the only mammals capable of powered flight. They are endlessly enchanting to watch as they perform agile flight manoeuvres in pursuit of their insect prey. People are often surprised to learn that there are seventeen breeding species of bat in the UK, at least eleven of which can be found in West London. What's more, several different species can be readily found close to our homes. The species can be separated to some extent using simple visual clues such as size, wing shape, flight pattern and height, and whether the bat is flying close to vegetation or out in the open.

Alongside powered flight, another remarkable ability that bats possess is their highly sophisticated system of echolocation. By emitting ultrasonic calls several times per second and listening to the returning echoes, bats form a highly detailed "sound picture" of their environment, enabling them to navigate through the landscape in the dark and locate their insect prey. With the aid of a bat detector, a hand-held electronic device, their ultrasonic calls can be converted to our audible range or recorded for computer analysis. The simplest type of bat detector is a heterodyne detector which has a dial enabling you to tune into the different frequencies at which different species echolocate. Initially tuning to 25 kHz will enable you to pick up the calls of our bigger bat species which echolocate at relatively low frequencies, such as noctule and serotine, while tuning to 50 kHz will pick up the calls of smaller species such as pipistrelles.

When going out looking for bats at night, it is important to take safety measures such as bringing someone with you and keeping an eye out for hazards – like the water! While a torch is essential for illuminating the ground in front of you, it should not be shone at the bats, and is best turned off when you are standing still for a better chance of seeing them.

Common pipistrelle (*Pipistrellus pipistrellus*), and soprano pipistrelle (*P. pygmaeus*), are the species you are most likely to spot. They are our smallest bats with a wingspan of up to 25 cm. Their flight is very agile with lots of twists and turns, often flying

A pipistrelle bat in flight. Photo: Barracuda

back and forth just above our head height along treelines or hedges. Both species can be found in a wide range of habitats including gardens, though soprano pipistrelles show a strong preference for foraging in wetland habitats so are particularly abundant along the Thames. Nathusius' pipistrelle (*P. nathusii*), is less abundant though still regularly recorded in West London. In fact, London is a hot spot for this species, particularly in the late summer and early autumn when the UK sees an influx of Nathusius' pipistrelles migrating from their main breeding grounds in Eastern Europe. Nathusius' pipistrelles have a strong association with large water bodies and are therefore regularly recorded along the Thames. They fly in more open environments than our other two resident pipistrelle species.

Three of our bigger bat species – the noctule (*Nyctalus noctula*), the Leisler's bat, (*N. leisleri*) and the serotine (*Eptesicus serotinus*), are found in West London, though serotines have become increasingly rare in recent years. The noctule is the UK's largest breeding species, with long, narrow, wings up to 40 cm in span. It flies out in the open, high above the trees, performing steep swoops when diving for prey. Leisler's bats are very similar to the noctule, though somewhat smaller with a wingspan up to 32 cm. They also forage out in the open, though typically not as high up, generally around tree-top height or lower, and perform shallower swoops after their prey. Serotines are a similar size to the noctule but have much broader wings which enable highly manoeuvrable flight close to vegetation and in tight circles when foraging in the open.

The remaining five species known to occur in West London are the Daubenton's bat (*Myotis daubentonii*), the Natterer's bat (*M. nattereri*), the whiskered bat, (*M. mystacinus*), the Brandt's bat (*M. brandtii*), and the brown long-eared bat (*Plecotus auritus*). The four Myotis species are usually difficult to distinguish, based on their calls alone, but Daubenton's bats can be recognised in flight by their distinctive habit of foraging close to the surface of water; they are regularly seen on the Thames and other bodies of water. Whiskered and Brandt's bats (the two species are frequently lumped together due to difficulties separating them) are rare species in West London, with only a handful of recorded sightings in recent decades. The Natterer's bat has broad wings which allow for highly manoeuvrable flight, including the ability to hover and glean invertebrates off vegetation. The same is true for the brown long-eared bat which is further distinguished by its huge ears. Brown long-eared bats tend to be under-recorded where they occur, as you need to be within a few metres to pick up their incredibly quiet echolocation calls on a bat detector. They are strongly associated with mature woodland and favour locations with very low to zero light levels, meaning that visual sightings of this species are rare. While all bat species are sensitive to lighting to differing extents, the above four species are particularly light-averse, limiting their distribution in London to locations with little to no light pollution.

Starting from Vauxhall Bridge and heading west along the river, the first outstanding site for bats is Battersea Park. Coincidentally just around the corner from the headquarters of the UK's national bat conservation charity, the Bat Conservation Trust, the park is virtually guaranteed to have high levels of bat activity on evenings with suitable weather conditions. Activity is highest around the lake, with the common pipistrelle the most abundant species. Soprano pipistrelles, Nathusius' pipistrelles, noctules, Leisler's bats, and Daubenton's bats are also regularly recorded.

Heading into the borough of Richmond-Upon-Thames, we come to Barnes which is home to the WWT London Wetland Centre. This site supports nationally important levels of soprano pipistrelle activity and it is also a regular site for common pipistrelles, Nathusius' pipistrelles (in the autumn males have been recorded producing their elaborate mating calls in the hope of attracting passing females), Daubenton's bats, noctules and Leisler's bats. Year-round monitoring has shown that the site has extensive bat activity even in the winter months, during spells of milder weather. The London Wetland Centre has a purpose-built, highly stylised bat house, the winning entry in a design competition instigated by Turner Prize-winner Jeremy Deller. The site usually closes before dusk, but a programme of evening public bat walks is run most years. Another important bat site close to the Thames in Barnes is the Leg O' Mutton Reservoir, which has a

Pump House in Battersea Park. Photo: John Chalmers

Aerial view of London Wetland Centre. Photo: LWC

similar bat fauna to the London Wetland Centre. This site is always open to the public.

Kew Gardens, with its rich variety of trees and plants and extensive areas of water and woodland is, unsurprisingly, an excellent site for bats. Some years ago, the Minka House was discovered to have a brown long-eared bat roost, with scatterings of dropp-ings and feeding remains (discarded moth wings) often easy to spot on the floor inside the house. Syon Park too offers important habitat for bats, though both these sites tend to close before dusk. Nearby, Old Deer Park offers extensive riverside bat habitat that has permanent public access.

Beyond Richmond bridge, continuing along the Twickenham side of the river, Warren Footpath is the site of an innovative project in 2010 which replaced the existing streetlights with more environmentally friendly LED lights designed to have a lower impact on bats. The lights are kept dimmed down to a low level, only brightening briefly in response to someone approaching along the footpath, and with reduced light spill onto the river and surrounding trees. Bat monitoring before and after the installation of the new lighting appeared to show that Daubenton's bats were starting to increase their foraging activity on the Thames in the vicinity of the Warren Footpath, a good sign that this side of the river was becoming more suitable for species that rely on darker habitats. A range of bat species are found along this stretch of the river, both along the footpath and in the grounds of Marble Hill Park and Orleans House.

The opposite side of the river, starting from Petersham Meadows and continuing past Ham House, is one of the darkest stretches of the Thames, and consequently has very high levels of bat activity with all of West London's species in evidence, including more elusive species such as Natterer's bats and brown long-eared bats which no doubt commute down the hill from Richmond Park where they are known to breed. Serotines have been recorded foraging over the cattle pasture on Petersham Meadows in the past, likely attracted by dung beetles which are among their preferred prey items. Ham Lands is an important extent of rich bat habitat that also has open public access, while the nearby Thames Young Mariners site supports a range of species including Nathusius' pipistrelles.

Heading into Kingston-Upon-Thames, a highly important riverside site is Seething Wells which has had ten bat species recorded on site or on the adjacent riverside, including the discovery of a Daubenton's bat maternity roost. Sadly, this site has been under recurring pressure for development in recent years. Canbury Gardens also supports high bat diversity and activity. Across the river – back into Richmond-Upon-Thames – Home Park, Hampton Court and Bushy Park form a large extent of bat habitat that is among the richest in London. Bushy Park has breeding populations of several species including Daubenton's bats, Natterer's bats, brown long-eared bats and (in one year at least) Nathusius' pipistrelles.

Gilbert White, in his celebrated book *The Natural History of Selborne* (first published 1788-9), described a summer evening's boat trip from Richmond to Sunbury, during which he saw large numbers of bats: "the air swarmed with them all along the Thames, so that hundreds were in sight at a time". While bats can still be seen in good numbers

The Minka House at Kew Gardens. Photo: Kew Gardens

Common noctule. Photo: Kamran Safi

along this stretch of the Thames, it seems clear that their abundance has diminished significantly in the two centuries since Gilbert White made his observations.

There is evidence from other parts of Britain that bat populations have declined, with the biggest changes thought to have occurred in the last hundred years. A few species are showing signs of recovery, thanks to the legal protection of bats and their roosts since 1981 and the activities of bat conservationists. However, many pressures remain, not least the impact of lighting and development. The Thames in West London is a highly important wildlife corridor that is very sensitive to such pressures and is subject to many planning applications along its banks. We can help by commenting on planning applications and pointing out where the impacts on bats and other wildlife have not been sufficiently considered. Where development is proposed in locations that are currently less rich in wildlife this can be an opportunity to incorporate provision for nature and potentially create links between London's more fragmented green spaces.

Rows of gardens provide wildlife corridors for bats and other animals. We can help by keeping our gardens dark at night and including features such as ponds and night-scented flowers that will attract insects for bats to feed on.

Buildings and mature trees may contain bat roosts so we should consider the possible presence of bats when planning any works that may cause damage or disturbance to roosts. We can also become members of organisations such as the Bat Conservation Trust and London Bat Group, thereby supporting their valuable work and discovering more about these fascinating mammals.

For information and advice on bats, see the Bat Conservation Trust (www.bats.org.uk). London Bat Group (www.londonbats.org.uk) is a voluntary group which works to protect and enhance London's bat populations.

Habitats & Heritage (www.habitatsandheritage.org.uk) supports bat conservation as part of its remit to care for the natural and historic environment and climate in South and West London.

Right: Dark walk by Petersham Meadows, a perfect habitat for bats. Photo: Carole Ratcliffe

"IN NATURE, NOTHING IS PERFECT AND EVERYTHING IS PERFECT. TREES CAN BE CONTORTED, BENT IN WEIRD WAYS, AND THEY'RE STILL BEAUTIFUL."

– Alice Walker

Sunrise over Leg O' Mutton pond. Photo: Sue Lindenberg

Delightfully varied habitats: pond, meadow, and forest at the top of Poor's Field

RUISLIP WOODS, HILLINGDON

Ian Alexander

Ruislip's woods are ancient, and on a quiet day the visitor can easily get the feeling of having stepped back in time, away from road and aircraft noise, and, deep in the woods, out of sight of any buildings. One of the strangest things about the woods to modern eyes, is the way the trees are being managed: by the medieval practice of coppicing. A modern forest planted for timber consists of trees all of the same kind, and all of the same age: when they're big enough, they're cut down and new trees are planted. A medieval forest isn't like that at all. It begins from a wildwood, a mixture of trees of different species. Much of Ruislip Woods consists of oak/hornbeam forest, about half of this is coppiced, meaning that the trees are cut down leaving a stump, or 'stool', above the ground. This rejuvenates the tree, causing new shoots to grow in a ring from the stool; stools may live for as long as five hundred years. The ring of shoots gets wider each time.

In medieval times, most of the trees were coppiced, leaving a few good straight 'Standards' to grow longer, perhaps for one hundred years or more. The Standards provided large timbers for house or ship beams, while the coppice provided firewood and materials for smaller carpentry.

Coppicing is on a 20-year cycle for each section. One section is coppiced each year, so that there are trees at every age between one and twenty somewhere in the coppiced woods, allowing different flowering plants, insects, and birds to flourish, each in the habitat they prefer. The other half of the woods is left uncoppiced, so there are many older trees.

The area became forested when the last Ice Age ended some 8,000 years ago. Like much of Southeast England, the succession to Wildwood ended with a mixed oak and hornbeam forest. Humans began to use the woods in the Bronze Age, hunting with spears, making pots, and living in small villages.

William the Conqueror gave the manor and woods of Ruislip, to one of his warriors, Ernulf de Hesdin, after the Norman Conquest in 1066. It was one of the most valuable of the more than twenty manors (including Newbury and Chipping Norton) granted to de Hesdin, suggesting that he had been a particularly useful warrior in the Norman Conquest. He made a gift of the manor to Normandy's Bec Abbey in 1087, perhaps out of piety. Over the next few centuries, the abbey used the woods to provide timber for many of London's ancient buildings: the Tower of London, the Palace of Westminster, and the Black Prince's Kennington manor house among them.

In 1451, King Henry VI granted the manor and the associated 'Lord of the Manor' title to King's College, Cambridge, which retained it until the 20th century. The local council planned to clear the woods and build thousands of homes on the land in 1914, but the First World War put a stop to the scheme. In 1931, King's College sold Park Wood to the local council, on condition that it was maintained as a wood rather than being built over. Soon afterwards, in 1936, both Copse Wood and Mad Bess Wood were combined with Park Wood, forming Ruislip Woods as we know it today. The story runs that 'Mad Bess' was the wife of a gamekeeper who lost her wits and spent her nights prowling the woods hunting for poachers. History does not relate what she did when she caught them.

The land didn't change ownership again until 1905, when Josef Conn obtained a lease from King's College and built a mansion in Copse Wood. It was purchased and luxuriously furnished by the shipping tycoon Meyer Franklin Kline in 1920. He sold the lease to a German, but in 1939, with the outbreak of war, the British government took the house over. It let the US Army's Clandestine Operations Division use the secluded property to train sabotage agents for secret missions in German-occupied France. The house burnt down in 1984.

A large Oak tree (a Standard) in Ruislip's Park Wood, with a thicket of young trees showing the area was recently coppiced

Hornbeam coppice stool with many new shoots in the fittingly named Copse Wood

In 1997, Ruislip Woods became London's first National Nature Reserve; the woods are also a Site of Special Scientific Interest. Its 305 hectares make it the largest woodland in Greater London, comprising Park Wood to the east and south, Poor's Field and Copse Wood to the north, and North Riding Wood, Mad Bess Wood, and Young Wood to the west. Park Wood is one of England's biggest areas of ancient semi-natural forest. The woods are actively managed for diversity, under the 100-year vision set out in the Long Term Management Plan, meant to maintain the woods in good condition both for public enjoyment and for nature, and protecting them against harmful activities like dumping, burning, and off-road driving.

The woods are London's richest in tree-living lichens. They are among the best places for bats in London, as they provide habitat and roost sites away from night-time disturbance are therefore valuable.

The woods hold at least 585 species of fungi, from edible kinds to handsome but tough brackets and dangerous toadstools. The picking of all wild fungi is prohibited; in a National Nature Reserve where fungi are critical to the woodland ecology, it's punishable by an enormous fine of up to £20,000. The risk of mixing a death cap into a mushroom sauce ought to be enough to put most people off – there's no antidote – but scientists have noticed that in areas subject to heavy collection, fungi are declining. Another reason not to pick fungi is simply that they are beautiful and interesting. If you see some in a wood, it's nice to leave them for other visitors to enjoy, and even photograph.

The grassland areas have to be managed to prevent them from turning into scrub and then forest. Rather than mowing, the grass of Poor's Field is grazed by Longhorn Cattle. They nip any tree seedlings in the bud, allowing a rich mixture of grasses and wildflowers to grow.

Longhorn Cattle managing the grassland of Poor's Field

Woody species include beech, sessile oak and English oak, as well as a rich variety of smaller trees such as aspen and rowan. The roots of beech and oak appear to compete for nutrients including nitrates in the soil, and it seems that beech is often able to exclude oak on soils that favour the beech. It is therefore unusual to find beech and oak growing together.

Ruislip Woods are an excellent place to see Britain's woodland birds, such as our three species of woodpeckers and the extraordinarily long-beaked woodcock. The woodcock is extremely well-camouflaged, so you're most likely to see one if you disturb it – it'll fly up making a startlingly loud noise with its wings. In spring, the males perform their "roding" flight above the trees soon after sunset, patrolling their territories and making odd squeaking and grunting calls to attract the females.

The reserve's woodland flowers include bugle and the imposing yellow archangel, both of which like shady places under the forest canopy. Both species readily spread with runners, making them pushy garden plants in their cultivated forms. If the runners are broken by trampling hooves or rootling snouts – a likely event in a wild wood – the separated plantlets quickly grow into new plants. In sunnier spots like Poor's Field, there is heathland, with ling heather and dwarf gorse, along with flowers uncommon in London like pignut and spotted orchid. Among the grasses is the delicate-looking fescue; its slender leaves are rolled up so they look like tiny cylinders. This may help the plants conserve water as the free-draining sandy soil can become very dry in summertime.

The woods and meadows host a rich variety of insects including many moths, some of them

Yellow Archangel in Park Wood

The day-flying Nettle-tap moth in Poor's Field

day-flying like the Burnet, coloured red and black to warn off predators, and the tiny but pretty Nettle-tap. In the woods you might glimpse the bright red of a scurrying Cardinal beetle, looking like an overgrown ladybird when it takes flight.

The woods are the home of numerous badgers, though as they're nocturnal, visitors are most likely to see signs like narrow paths that disappear under low vegetation, parallel scratch marks on trees from their sharp claws, or the multiple tunnel-openings of their underground dens or setts.

Next to the woods is Ruislip Lido, a former reservoir in a beautiful natural setting. It was built in 1811 by the Scottish engineer John Rennie to provide water for the Grand Union Canal. It became a lido in 1933.

Ruislip Lido is now a popular place for sunbathing, walks, boating, and paddling, with a charming miniature steam railway that goes much of the way around both sides of the lake, giving close-up views of the beautiful woods and waterside.

All photos courtesy of Ian Alexander

Swans on Ruislip Lido, created to supply water for the Grand Union Canal

European robin at Chiswick House. Photo: James Yates

A view of the Thames from Richmond Hill. Photo: panoramio

THE UPPER THAMES ESTUARY

Wanda Bodnar

The River Thames is one of the most well-known rivers in the world. It rises from a group of springs at Cotswold Hills in Gloucestershire and meanders its way through southern England via Cricklade, Oxford, Wallingford, and Reading, amongst other places. It enters Greater London at Hampton Court and carries on from Teddington for about 95 miles to the east, joining the North Sea at Shoeburyness in Essex and Sheerness in Kent. This 95-mile section of the River Thames east of Teddington is what we refer to as the tidal Thames or the Thames Estuary. This is London's biggest open space.

Because of its connection to the sea, the Thames Estuary has two high tides and two low tides each day, with a tidal range of up to seven metres. Thanks to this non-stop movement of the river, the naturally occurring mud on the riverbed is constantly resuspended, mixed, and moved around within the water. If you ever looked at the Thames closely from above, you would notice a continuously moving layer of brown clouds. This brown colour is often seen as a sign of pollution, however, the river has always been this colour. Our contemporary name even comes from the Latin name Tamesis, meaning darkness.

Mud is an important element of a healthy aquatic ecosystem. It is a combination of soil, silt, and clay, and it contains important inorganic nutrients (such as nitrate, ammonium, and phosphate). These are released into the water with each tidal cycle, stimulating plankton growth. This makes the Thames Estuary an incredibly productive aquatic ecosystem supporting many species, including over 115 species of fish, two species of seals, harbour porpoise, and 92 species of birds.

With the constant flow of freshwater from upstream and from the tributaries, as well as saltwater intrusion from the sea, different sections of the Thames Estuary have different salt content. The upper reaches, between Teddington and Hammersmith, are predominantly freshwater with a very small amount of salt from the sea. Here, fish species found include bream (*Abramis brama*), roach (*Rutilus rutilus*), dace (*Leuciscus leuciscus*), grayling (*Thymallus thymallus*), and pike (*Esox lucius*). At this section, the river runs through a leafy, open stretch of historic landscape lined with wet woodlands, reedbeds and gravelly foreshore. There are also several islands (often called aits or eyots) dotted throughout. There are about 180 of these river islands on the entire stretch of the River Thames, with nine on the Thames Estuary.

The largest of these, just below Teddington, is Eel Pie Island. Its name dates back

The Eel Pie pub in Twickenham. Photo: Jim Linwood

to the Tudor period when eel pies were made at the local inn. Legend has it that Henry VIII found them so delicious he insisted on the first pie of each season.

Interestingly, fishermen on the Thames always distinguished between the European eel (*Anguilla anguilla*), and "fish." This was most likely because during the medieval period eels took up about 50% of the fish biomass. Eels were then used as currency and were also a good source of protein and fat, especially for London's poor. They were also a favourite during Lent due to the long-held belief that they reproduced asexually.

There is still very little known about eels. No one has ever observed eels mating in captivity or the wild and their spawning ground in the Sargasso Sea was not discovered until the 1920s. Nevertheless, it is believed that eels spawn via external fertilisation: females release millions of eggs into the water where they are fertilised by the male's sperm. The eggs then hatch into a larval form called leptocephalae and using the currents they drift across the Atlantic Ocean into European rivers, including the Thames Estuary and its freshwater tributaries. Once here, they start their metamorphosis, first into glass eels, then into elvers, before growing and maturing into yellow, and finally, silver eels. After about twenty years living in freshwater rivers, silver eels make their transatlantic journey back into the Sargasso Sea where they spawn and die.

Eels are still found in a wide variety of freshwater and estuarine habitats, however, since the 1980s, adult populations have decreased by over 90% across Europe and are now classified as 'Critically Endangered' by the IUCN (International Union for Conservation of Nature).

Further downstream from Eel Pie Island we can find the Victorian-built Richmond half-tide lock. The Old London Bridge, which stood for over six hundred years from 1209 until 1831, was a thick stone-built bridge with nineteen wide bridge footings, or piers. These piers greatly restricted the tidal movement of the river effectively turning the bridge into a dam. After the Old London Bridge was demolished and rebuilt with much wider arches, river levels in Richmond would significantly drop with the outgoing tide. To stop the river draining away twice a day, the Richmond half-tide lock was built in 1894. The lock has three vertical steel sluice gates that are suspended from a footbridge. These gates are raised for around two hours each side of high tide. The rest of the day the gates remain closed to hold the water levels at half tide. This allows river navigation between Richmond and Teddington to be maintained and also provides a stable habitat for wildlife.

Every year for a few weeks in Autumn, the sluice gates remain lifted, letting the river drain away with the low tide and exposing the riverbed. During this 'draw-off' volunteers organise litter picks, mudlarks look for treasures and the Zoological Society of London (ZSL) carries out its annual Thames Invasive Species Survey.

The Thames is a highly invaded ecosystem. Common vectors that transport aquatic non-native species include ballast water from ships and fishing gear. Notable invasive species in the Thames are the Chinese mitten crab (*Eriocheir sinensis*), quagga mussel (*Dreissena bugensis*), zebra mussel (*Dreissena polymorpha*) and the Asian clam (*Corbicula fluminea*). The latter three can rapidly reproduce and have the potential to significantly alter entire ecosystems by outcompeting native species. In a survey carried out in 2017, the Asian clam accounted for 79% of the total mussels counted.

Our next stop is Isleworth Ait, another one of the beautiful river islands. Isleworth Ait is designated as a nature reserve (overseen by the London Wildlife Trust), providing sanctuary for more than 50 species of birds and two rare species of air-breathing land snails: the German hairy snail (*Pseudotrichia rubiginosa*) and the Thames door snail

Richmond half-tide lock. Photo: Wanda Bodnar

Syon Park from the river. Photo: Wanda Bodnar

(*Balea biplicata*). Except for a small colony in Purfleet, Essex, the Thames door snail lives almost exclusively on Isleworth Ait.

Slightly further along the river is Syon Park. It is connected to a larger expanse of green space, including Kew Gardens and Richmond Park, linked by the Thames Estuary. Syon Park's most significant feature is the undisturbed tidal meadow that floods at each high tide. This meadow is one of the few remaining Thames-side wetland areas and the only natural riverbank on the Thames Estuary. It is classified as a Site of Special Scientific Interest (SSSI). Species living here include bats, invertebrates, birds, fungi, and lichen. Chinese mitten crabs can also be found here in the soft mud of the riverbank.

The Chinese mitten crab first appeared in the Thames in the 1930s. Just like the European eels, they are catadromous species which means that they spend their lives in freshwater rivers, but they migrate to the sea to spawn. In late summer, female adult crabs move into fully saline waters where they lay up to a million eggs. After the eggs hatch, the larvae migrate back into brackish and freshwater areas where they develop into juvenile and adult crabs.

The Chinese mitten crab is listed as one of the world's worst invasive species as it can tolerate a wide range of environmental conditions, reproduce quickly, and has few natural predators. They are especially a nuisance in the Thames as they can create complex, interconnected burrows which can lead to riverbank erosion and ultimately to habitat loss.

Chinese mitten crab in Deptford. Photo: Neil Cummings

Located between Kew Bridge and Kew Rail Bridge, Oliver's Island derives its name from the story that Oliver Cromwell once took refuge here in 1642 during the Battle of Brentford in the First English Civil War. It was rumoured that Cromwell was trapped in the nearby Bull's Head Pub, having escaped to the island via a secret tunnel. Today the island is covered with willows and poplars providing a breeding ground for birds such as herons, cormorants, and Canada geese. Occasionally, seals can also be spotted basking in the sun opposite the island, on the foreshore of the picturesque Strand-on-the-Green.

Seals are perhaps the most exciting creatures to encounter on the Thames. The two resident seal species are the common or harbour seal (*Phoca vitulina*), and the grey seal (*Halichoerus grypus*). They can be easily distinguished by their head and nose features: harbour seals have short muzzles with V-shaped nostrils, and grey seals are much more dog-like with their hooked nose and parallel nostrils.

Both common and grey seals have a well-developed sense of vision and hearing. Their vision is specifically adapted to see in dark and murky waters and their whiskers are particularly powerful as they can detect the movement of their favourite meal (eels, flatfish,

Harbour seal near Oliver's Island. Photo: Wanda Bodnar

and invertebrates) as far as 100 metres. Apart from their head and flippers, their body is well insulated with a thick layer of blubber or fat. Their flippers have a dense network of blood vessels just under the skin and are used to regulate their body temperature when out of the water. To avoid getting too cold, they can shut off the blood circulation close to their skin and lift their head and flippers, taking up their signature banana-shaped pose. To avoid getting too warm, they simply dangle their head and flippers into the water and utilise blood circulation to cool their body.

Common seals are more normally spotted hauled out on the Thames foreshore during the spring and summer months as this is when they mate, breed, nurse their pup and go through their annual moult. The grey seals, on the other hand, spend most of their time at sea, only coming to shore along the coast during the winter months.

Aerial seal surveys, carried out annually by the Zoological Society of London (ZSL), indicate that the population of these wonderful marine animals is improving with an estimate of 900 harbour seals and 3200 grey seals living in the Thames Estuary today. Therefore, it is important to consider that both species can be encountered along the Thames foreshore. When hauled out, they are simply getting warm or resting while digesting their food so it is best to leave them undisturbed and to keep your dog on a leash when near to them. In fact, the best way to enjoy their company is to keep them completely unaware of human presence.

Chiswick Eyot is the last of the river islands on the Thames, and it has a dense vegetation of willow trees and reedbeds. Chiswick Mall was at one time a famous fishery with species such as perch, barbel, smelt, eels and salmon frequently caught.

The Thames used to be a productive salmon (*Salmo salar*) river and, just like eels, salmon was once used to pay rent, especially by fishermen. However, eels, salmon and other fish stocks had significantly declined due to the deteriorating water quality in the past and the construction of weirs and navigational locks. According to C. J. Cornish, the last salmon was caught between Chiswick Eyot and Putney in 1812. Between 1975 and 2008 there had been several attempts to restock the Thames with juvenile salmon, however, the water quality of the river is no longer suitable to support them.

Even though it has gone through periods of decline and recovery due to farming, residential and industrial development, the Thames is one of the world's cleanest rivers running through a city. Thanks to the hard work of many, its water quality continues to improve. One aspect of this is the Tideway Tunnel, or London Super Sewer. Unwanted sewage spills, coming from London's ageing Victorian sewer system, are still a problem, and the 25km tunnel being built will capture and store raw sewage and rainwater. When it becomes operational it is expected that sewage overflows will decrease by 95%. With so much amazing wildlife already present, it will be exciting to see how aquatic life benefits and diversifies with this new structure.

For more visit: https://www.thamesestuarypartnership.org/

A seal in the vicinity of Eel Pie island. Photo: Mary Tester

Red Deer in Richmond Park. Photo: James Yates

Wimbledon Common. Photo: Amy Burgess

WIMBLEDON COMMON

Ian Alexander

Wimbledon Common is a large unenclosed area that serves as a park as well as a special place for nature. Footpaths, bridleways, cycle tracks, and the fairways of a golf course crisscross the area, inviting a wealth of outdoor activities. It contains the biggest piece of open heathland anywhere in London. On the hillsides that fall away to the west is a substantial area of semi-natural woodland, and there are nine man-made ponds including the medieval Rushmere, which provided bundles of rushes for thatching houses. There are spacious sports grounds at the northwest and southwest corners of the common. To the south is the graceful Cannizaro Park, with its formal Italian Garden, lawns, statues, and azalea dell as well as many beautiful trees.

The common's name gives a clue to its origin. Unlike the adjoining area of Richmond Park, which was a private royal hunting-ground, Wimbledon Common was always open to the public. For centuries, the local commoners had rights to graze their animals, to dig for peat or sand, to catch fish, and to take heather, bracken, rushes, and wood (but not to fell trees) for their own use, even though the land might belong to a noble lord. In the 1860s, the Lord of the Manor was Earl Spencer, who attempted to enclose 700 acres, most of the common, as his private park. The commoners, led by the biscuit-maker Henry Peek, took him to court and successfully asserted their common rights. As a result, Spencer set up a trust to manage the common as an open space for the public.

Wimbledon Common - 18th century houses of West Place (Fox & Grapes pub on left) in a landscape. Photo: Ian Alexander

Creeping Willow. Photo: Ian Alexander

Interesting structures on the common include, towards the north, a traditional windmill, which hosts a tearoom and a small museum, and to the south the remains of an Iron Age hill fort. The fort is now named 'Caesar's Camp': it was active half a millennium earlier than Julius Caesar's invasion of Britain, but was probably captured by the Romans a century after Caesar, when Claudius invaded Britain.

The common, including 'Putney Heath' and Putney Lower Common (neither of which are in Putney), covers some 460 hectares or 1100 acres. Its importance to nature is marked by two nature reserves, a Site of Special Scientific Interest, and a Special Area of Conservation. The whole area is a Site of Metropolitan Importance for Nature Conservation. The open areas consist of heath, meaning that the purple-flowered ling heather is the dominant plant, along with rarer species of heather, and unusual woody plants like creeping willow.

The heath is accompanied by acid grassland, where purple moor-grass abounds on the lime-poor sands and gravels. Many other grasses and flowers are mixed in with these. An important flowering plant is the yellow rattle, named for the way its seeds rattle inside their ripe pods when shaken. Its value interestingly lies in the way it weakens the taller and tougher grasses, as it is partly parasitic on their roots. The result is that the grass cover is thinned out, allowing many species of smaller flowering plants to move in. These include the little yellow cross-shaped flowers of tormentil; the pretty red and yellow flowers of birdsfoot trefoil or 'bacon and eggs'; and the tiny white stars of heath bedstraw. Overall, more than a hundred kinds of flowering plant live on the common. A similar number of bird species have been recorded; among the birds of prey are the dramatically scythe-winged hobby and buzzard as well as kestrel and sparrowhawk, while tawny owls can be heard hooting as darkness falls.

Wimbledon Common is a good place for butterflies and moths, with a chance of glimpsing rarities like purple emperor and green hairstreak. It's a special place for dragonflies, too, with at least 20 species recorded on the waters of the common, including Queensmere, Bluegate

Yellow Iris on the common.
Photo: Ian Alexander

Pond, Hookhamslade Pond and the Beverley Brook, which forms the western edge of the common. Some dragonflies like the southern hawker can travel quite far from their breeding ponds, and may be found on warm summer days sunning themselves out on the moor. With its many old trees, the Common is an important place for one of our largest insects, the stag beetle. The adults, including the males with their impressive antler-like mandibles, only live for a few weeks. The rest of the life-cycle is underground, as the larvae burrow for as much as seven years in dead wood, preferring it when it's partly buried. Visitors may be puzzled to see a rotten log torn to sawdusty shreds: foxes use their keen noses to locate the plump larvae, digging into the wood for an easy meal.

The mammals of the common include foxes, rabbits, weasels, and badgers, as well as ten species of bat. The ponds are home to common frogs and toads, smooth newts, and the red-eared slider (an accidentally introduced terrapin, the wild population having bred from released pets). The heath's reptiles are the common lizard and the grass snake. The latter, whilst non-poisonous, will often hiss and pretend to strike when it is picked up; it also will spray smelly liquids from its anal glands, or even pretend to be dead. Understandably, it's better left on its own.

The Common contains the Fishponds Wood and Beverley Meads local nature reserve, considered important for nature conservation. Fishpond Wood is unusual in combining an area of mature oak-hazel woodland with two seasonal ponds that support a wealth of wildlife, including many hundreds of frogs. To the west and south is Beverley Meads, four small acid grassland meadows particularly good for herbaceous plants and butterflies, surrounded by scrub and woodland. Management involves some desilting and controls emergent vegetation in the ponds, to prevent them from filling in and turning into woodland, and clears invading scrub to keep the meadows open. Analysis of the pollen in layers of silt in Fishpond Wood, to a depth of four metres, shows that the area was open wet grassland while the local mill was in use. It was a fulling mill, meaning that it cleaned and

Conservation work at Farm Bog: a dead-hedge inhibits walkers, while trees have been cut back. Photo: Ian Alexander

Ribbonwort. Photo: John Game

matted woollen cloth. The mill burnt down sometime around 1520, and the amount of shrub and tree pollen gradually increased in the upper layers of silt, implying that the area was abandoned and became more wooded, as it is today.

Amidst the bustle and crowds, Wimbledon Common holds a secret. Near its southern edge (to the east of Fishponds Wood) is a small oasis of peace and quiet, where a rare habitat supports some special plants, insects, and mammals: Farm Bog. Not long after the end of the last Ice Age, a slight hollow in the ground formed a wet area, perhaps a shallow pond, about a hectare in extent. Mosses started to grow. Over the next 6,000 years or so, the sphagnum moss flourished on the wet ground, and layers of dead moss accumulated to a thickness of two metres or so: lowland peat. Because the moss is spongy, as it grows the material becomes able to hold more and more water, so the area stays wet. The groundwater here is acidic, and the peat forms a bog, a soft squelchy place where you shouldn't walk, both because you'll sink into the mud, and because the habitat is fragile.

Among the moss are plants that are now as uncommon as lowland bogs, like bladderwort and bogbean. A speciality is ribbonwort, a flat green ribbonlike plant with no leaves that grows on wet ground. Farm Bog, now a local nature reserve, is one of just two places in London where it still finds the habitat it needs. There are some less than usual animals too, such as the common lizard, the water shrew, and the wasp spider.

Farm Bog has been maintained since the 1980s. The task is the boggy equivalent of regularly mowing a meadow to stop it turning into forest: to clear reeds, scrub, and creeping brambles each year, to stop the bog turning into wet woodland. Along with the other wet areas, it provides a wonderful glimpse of a wild wetland. Wedged between a busy main road and a densely built-up suburb, Wimbledon Common allows dog walkers, picnickers, and other visitors to experience some really wild corners and diverse natural habitats in the heart of Southwest London.

Nature on Wimbledon and Putney Commons: https://www.wpcc.org.uk/nature/nature
Cannizaro Park: https://www.cannizaropark.com/

Hookhamslade Pond, Wimbledon Common. Photo: Andy Scott

Red Deer Hinds walking through the mist at sunrise, Bushy Park. Photo: Sue Lindenberg

"IT IS IN THE WILD PLACES, WHERE THE EDGE OF THE EARTH MEETS THE CORNERS OF THE SKY, THE HUMAN SPIRIT IS FED."

– Art Wolfe

Eurasian Coot in Kew Gardens. Photo: James Yates

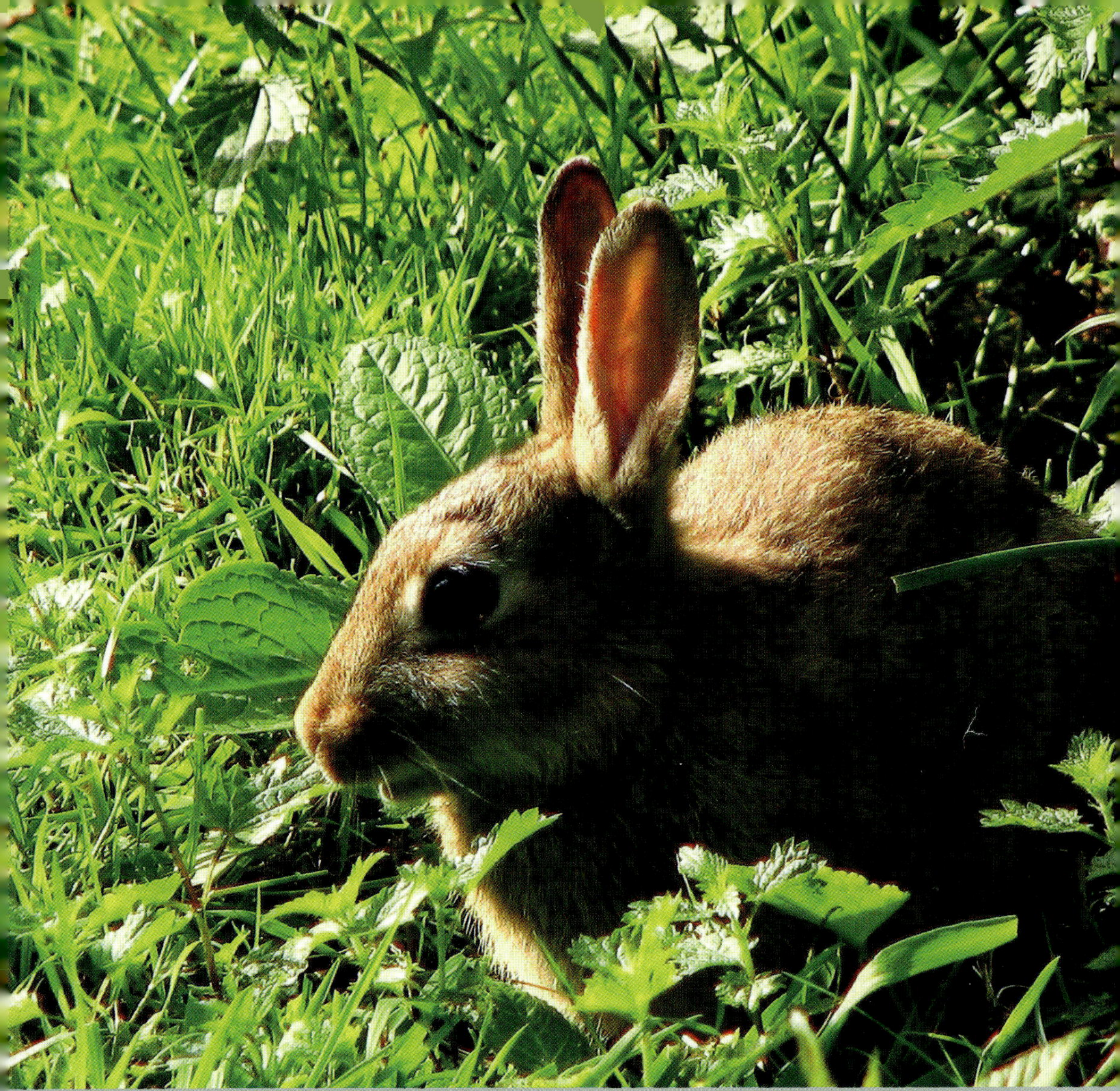

Wild rabbit on Hampstead Heath. Photo: Garry Knight